A GUIDE FOR DEVELOPING, WRITING & IMPLEMENTING SCIENTIFIC RESEARCH GRANT PROPOSALS

Edited by Clete A. Kushida, MD, PhD

A Joint Publication of the American Academy of Sleep Medicine and the Sleep Research Society

Copies of the book are available from the American Academy of Sleep Medicine (AASM) in the U.S.A. Correspondence regarding copyright permissions should be directed to the Executive Director, American Academy of Sleep Medicine, One Westbrook Corporate Center, Suite 920, Westchester, IL 60154, U.S.A. Translations to other languages must be authorized by the American Academy of Sleep Medicine, U.S.A.

Kushida, CA as editor for the American Academy of Sleep Medicine and Sleep Research Society. A Guide for Developing, Writing and Implementing Scientific Research Grant Proposals. Westchester, Illinois: American Academy of Sleep Medicine and Sleep Research Society, 2010. Soft cover. Includes Index.

Library of Congress Control Number: 2010901316

ISBN: 0-9657220-5-8

TABLE OF CONTENTS

List of Contributors **6**

Foreword by Michael Twery, PhD. **7**

Preface by Clete A. Kushida, MD, PhD. **11**

Chapter I—Introduction by Clete A. Kushida, MD, PhD. **13**

Chapter II—Funding Sources: Types and Description by M. Safwan Badr, MD. **15**
    Introduction 15
    Strategic Planning 15
    Research Fellowship Support. 16
    Institutional Funding Opportunities. 16
    Extramural Funding Opportunities 17
        Types of Research Awards. 17
        Sources of Funding 17
        How to Assess Potential Opportunities 18
    Summary 18
    Resources 19

Chapter III—Mentors, Collaborators, and Consultants by Sairam Parthasarathy, MD **21**
    Introduction 21
    Roles and Responsibilities of Mentors. 21
        Mentor-Mentee Relationship. 22
        Choosing and Interacting With a Mentor 23
        Beginner's Traps 25
        "What Do You Want?". 25
        Career Development Plan 26
    Advisory Committee 27
    Collaborators and Consultants 27
        Selection Process. 28
        Biosketches and Other Support. 29
    Institutional and Departmental Support 30
    Acknowledgements 30
    References 30
    Appendix A: Progress in Career Development Plan 31
    Appendix B: Mentorship Contract 32
    Appendix C: Mentor's Training Matrix 33
    Appendix D: Career Development Activities. 34
    Appendix E: Sample Biosketch 35

Chapter IV—Selecting the Research Question by Atul Malhotra, MD and Patrick J. Strollo, Jr., MD. **37**
    Before You Start. 37
    General Points 37
    Selecting the Outcomes and Specific Aims 38
    Literature Review. 39
    Preliminary Data 40
    Analyses. 40
    Other Sections of the Grant Proposal. 41
    Final Thoughts 42

Chapter V—Study Design for Human Studies by Terri Weaver, PhD and Connie M. Ulrich, PhD **43**
    Introduction 43
    Threats to Validity 43
    Types of Human Studies 46
        Survey Research 46
        Quasi-Experimental Designs. 46
        Experimental Designs 49
    Phases of Clinical Trials. 49
    Types of Randomization. 50
    Designs. 51

Baseline Assessment 52
Ethical Concerns 52
    What is Equipoise and Why is it Ethically Controversial? 53
    Placebos, Sham Interventions, and Blinding Procedures in Sleep Medicine 54
    Treatment Failures, Underpowered Studies, and External Monitoring. 56
    Summary 57
Statistical Concerns 57
    Sample Size Determination. 57
    Nonadherence 58
    Missing Data 59
    Early Study Termination 60
Summary 61
References 61

Chapter VI—Special Considerations for Animal and Translational Research by Seiji Nishino, MD, PhD **63**
Introduction 63
Considerations in the Selection of Animal Species and Models 64
    Gene Targeting and Genetically Modified Animals 66
        Random Mutagenesis 66
        Sleep Phenotype Variations and QTL 66
        Candidate Gene Approaches, Transgenic, Gene Knockout, Knock-In and Knockdown . . . 67
        General Considerations for Interpreting the Results Using Knock-Out and Transgenic Mice . . . 67
        Antisense Targeting and Gene Knockdown 68
    Simpler Animal Models. 68
    Existing Animal Models of Sleep Disorders 70
Study Design 70
Biosafety and Guidelines 72
Animal Facility and Veterinary Care Issues. 74
    Animal Environment 74
    Veterinary Care 75
Monitoring Procedures. 75
    Monitoring the Site Surrounding an Implanted Device 75
Procedural Considerations for Anesthesia, Restraint, and Euthanasia 76
    Anesthesia and Analgesia 76
    Multiple Major Surgical Procedures 76
    Pain and Distress 77
    Head-Restraint Systems. 77
    Sleep Deprivation 78
    Guidelines for Endpoint Monitoring and Humane Termination 79
    Euthanasia 79
References 80

Chapter VII—Writing the Grant Proposal by Clifford B. Saper, MD, PhD **85**
General Tips for Successful Grant Writing 85
Sections of the Grant Proposal. 86
    Abstract 86
    Specific Aims. 86
    Background and Significance 87
    Preliminary Data/Progress Report. 88
    Experimental Design 89
Revision and Resubmission 92

Chapter VIII—Developing Grant Budgets: How to Get What You Need by Phyllis C. Zee, MD, PhD. **95**
Introduction 95
Developing Your Budget 95
    Modular vs. Non-Modular Budget 95
    Total Cost = Direct + Indirect Costs 96
    Personnel and Salaries. 96
    Consultant Costs 98
    Equipment 98
    Supplies 98

Travel 98
   Patient Care Costs 98
   Other Expenses 99
Cost Escalation 101
Post Award Changes in Budget and No-Cost Extension 101
Summary and Conclusion 105
Resources 105

Chapter IX—The Grant Application Review Process by Mark R. Opp, PhD **107**
Introduction 107
The Submission 107
   Center for Scientific Review 107
   The Cover Letter 108
   Supplemental Materials 109
The Review 110
Scoring of the Application 112
The Study Section Meeting 113
   Study Section Composition and Attendees 113
   Meeting Agenda 114
   Asynchronous Electronic Discussion (AED) Review 114
   The Critique ("pink" sheet) 115
The Resubmission 116
Resources 118

Chapter X—Implementing the Grant Proposal by Clete A. Kushida, MD, PhD **119**
Study Organization and Timeline 119
Protocol and Manual of Operations Development 120
Study Oversight 120
   Steering Committee 120
   NIH Program Officer 121
   Data and Safety Monitoring Board (DSMB) 121
   Clinical Coordinating Center (CCC) 122
Personnel Training 122
Informed Consent 123
   Multicenter Considerations 123
   Genetic Testing 123
Participant Recruitment and Retention 123
Data Management 124
   Quality Assurance and Control 124
   Interim Analyses 125
   Data Sharing and Collaboration 125
   Data Coordinating Center Roles and Responsibilities 125
      Operations Core 125
      Biostatistics Core 126
      Data Management Core 127
   Efficacy Analyses of Primary and Secondary Outcomes 128
Participant Safety 129
   Adverse Event Monitoring and Reporting 129
   Participant Education to Mitigate Risks 129
   Medical Alerts 129
   Safety Officers 130
Performance Assessment and Adherence to Protocol and Timelines 130
Ancillary Studies 130
Publications and Presentations 131
Study Closeout 131
   Data Cleanup and Verification 131
   Data Storage 131
   Dissemination of Results and Data Reporting Guidelines 131
References 131

Index of Keywords **133**

LIST OF CONTRIBUTORS

EDITOR

Clete A. Kushida, MD, PhD
Director, Stanford Center for Human Sleep Research
Associate Professor, Stanford Medical Center
Stanford University School of Medicine
Palo Alto, California

AUTHORS

M. Safwan Badr, MD
Professor and Chief, Division of Pulmonary, Critical Care and Sleep Medicine
Wayne State University School of Medicine
Executive Vice President and Chief Medical Officer
Detroit Medical Center
Detroit, Michigan

Clete A. Kushida, MD, PhD
Director, Stanford Center for Human Sleep Research
Associate Professor, Stanford Medical Center
Stanford University School of Medicine
Palo Alto, California

Atul Malhotra, MD
Associate Professor of Medicine, Harvard Medical School
Clinical Chief of Division of Sleep Medicine, Department of Medicine
Medical Director of the Brigham Sleep Disorders Research Program
Pulmonary & Critical Care and Sleep Medicine Division
Brigham & Women's Hospital
Boston, Massachusetts

Seiji Nishino, MD, PhD
Professor, Psychiatry & Behavioral Sciences
Director, Sleep and Circadian Neurobiology Laboratory
Stanford University School of Medicine
Palo Alto, California

Mark R. Opp, PhD
Professor
Department of Anesthesiology
Department of Molecular and Integrative Physiology
Neuroscience Graduate Program
University of Michigan
Ann Arbor, Michigan

Sairam Parthasarathy, MD
Chief of Research
Southern Arizona VA Health Care System
Associate Professor of Medicine
University of Arizona College of Medicine
Tucson, Arizona

Clifford B. Saper, MD, PhD
James Jackson Putnam Professor of Neurology and Neuroscience
Harvard Medical School
Chairman, Department of Neurology
Beth Israel Deaconess Medical Center
Boston, Massachusetts

Patrick J. Strollo, Jr., MD, FCCP, FAASM
Medical Director
UPMC Sleep Medicine Center
Associate Professor of Medicine and Clinical and Translational
Science Division of Pulmonary, Allergy, and Critical Care Medicine
University of Pittsburgh Medical College
Pittsburgh, Pennsylvania

Connie M. Ulrich, PhD, RN, FAAN
Associate Professor of Bioethics and Nursing
Senior Fellow, Center for Bioethics, Department of Medical Ethics
Senior Fellow, Leonard Davis Institute of Economics
University of Pennsylvania School of Nursing
Philadelphia, Pennsylvania

Terri Weaver, PhD, RN, FAAN
Ellen and Robert Kapito Professor in Nursing
Science Chair
Biobehavioral and Health Sciences Division
University of Pennsylvania School of Nursing
Professor
Department of Medicine
Division of Sleep Medicine, School of Medicine
University of Pennsylvania
Philadelphia, Pennsylvania

Phyllis C. Zee, MD, PhD
Professor of Neurology and Neurobiology & Physiology
Director Sleep Disorders Center
Northwestern University Feinberg School of Medicine
Chicago, Illinois

The time for clinical research is now. In the field of sleep research, for instance, landmark advances in understanding sleep regulation, sleep disorders, and circadian biology have laid a strong foundation for launching a new era of clinical research and for advances in sleep disorders medicine. Tremendous progress elucidating basic pathways of sleep regulation and biological timing and characterizing populations at risk needs to be applied to the task of defining the specific opportunities where sleep disorder treatment reduces disease risk and improves disease outcomes. In light of recent momentum toward practicing evidence-based medicine, investigator-initiated studies are urgently needed to determine sleep disorder treatment efficacy and evaluate effectiveness in a wide range of disease contexts. Studies are also needed to compare the impact of existing therapeutic options, the relative benefits and risks of each option, barriers, and costs (comparative effectiveness research).

The evidence indicating that sleep disorders are pervasive and sleep deprivation is characteristic of modern urban lifestyles has never been stronger. An emerging challenge for clinical sleep research is to increase the pace at which new data sources are utilized, cross-cutting relationships analyzed, and findings reported. A vast array of new resources is available today through collaboration with studies such as the Sleep Heart Health Study and public datasets. The proliferation of electronic medical record systems with comprehensive, longitudinal records of individual encounters is opening unprecedented opportunities for research in support of evidence-based medicine. Existing datasets with sleep phenotypes are fertile testing grounds for novel hypothesis generation and the exploration of new relationships coupling sleep to specific intermediate markers of disease and basic behavioral and social risk factors. Leveraging these resources often requires teams of researchers representing clinical, biological, and bioinformatic domains of expertise to innovatively approach the highest priority questions and develop implementable research strategies. Temporal relationships influencing disease etiology, severity, and therapeutic outcomes are not well understood. Experts in sleep and circadian biology are uniquely positioned to make highly innovative contributions to biomedical research teams of the future.

As the world's largest public sponsor of investigator-initiated biomedical research, the National Institutes of Health supports studies with highly meritorious plans to improve our understanding of how the human body works and the potential to contribute to the goal of improving people's health, and save lives. In 2010, the NIH identified five areas of program emphasis that are intended to accelerate interdisciplinary approaches empowered by open access to tools, databases, and technologies. High-throughput analytical technologies are catalyzing efforts to define health and clinical disease phenotypes in terms of cellular function. Scientific advances linking circadian biology to fundamental cellular functions and pathophysiology in virtually every tissue and system suggests that there are many new discoveries awaiting clinical sleep research.

The translation of basic discoveries into new diagnostics and treatments is a second area of NIH emphasis. There is an immense need for clinical studies that apply what has been learned in terms of molecules, pathophysiology, and behavior to the development of new sustainable intervention strategies. Clinical sleep researchers can contribute uniquely to teams of investigators at every stage of the translational process leading to evidence-based medicine. What is known about the biology of sleep and sleep disorders needs to be juxtaposed with other considerations to inform the design of clinical trials, the assessment of physiological and psychological outcomes, and the interpretation of intervention safety, efficacy, and effectiveness.

Reinventing health care and global health are also NIH priorities to the extent that research can make substantial contributions. Sleep disorders and an array of closely-related co-morbid conditions are among the most pervasive chronic medical conditions, and contribute immensely to burdens on the health care system.

Epidemiological data indicates that chronic sleep deprivation as part of lifestyle choices also influences health care utilization. However, these relationships and the potential benefits of intervention are not well understood. Comparative effective research, the identification of individual genetic and environmental factors that modify disease risk, and health disparities research are directions of interest at the NIH that can help the stature of sleep disorders research and foster the process of health care reform in the nation.

The NIH is also placing a strong emphasis on overhauling processes that support the NIH biomedical research community. One focus is on new application formats and a redefinition of review criteria starting in fiscal year 2010 that will place greater emphasis on "innovation" in NIH peer review. A second focus is on increasing the robustness of training programs NIH-wide. An array of NIH funding mechanisms are available for clinical sleep researchers whether they are new, early stage investigators or mid-career investigators seeking to protect research time and mentoring or develop new research skills. Despite these opportunities, the number of positions available for "clinical research" training may be insufficient to support all of the best applicants and the number of faculty career opportunities available to the scientific workforce are likely to be limited. The NIH is considering new funding mechanisms that may help address some of these barriers to clinical research careers.

In this environment, new questions and medical opportunities emerging from recent advances in preclinical sleep and circadian studies may favor the competitive standing of clinical sleep research trainees and investigators who are well-informed about how the NIH is organized, and well-prepared to engage multidisciplinary and collaborative team research activities. Realizing the goal of leveraging NIH-funded program opportunities to attain competitive careers in clinical research ultimately lies with the individual investigator. Developing an understanding of your personal timeline of eligibility for various NIH funding mechanisms and opportunity windows may be a useful tool and starting point. The NIH consists of 27 separate Institutes and Centers that award grants. While there is considerable similarity across the NIH as a whole, it is critical to understand that each NIH funding component independently develops plans for the implementation of its scientific mission including the grant mechanisms that are supported, applicant eligibility, fiscal policy, and innumerable administrative factors influencing the consideration of applications. A general awareness of how your interests in clinical sleep research align with the current scientific agenda of various Institutes may reveal new funding opportunities or suggest new avenues of investigation. In fiscal year 2009, NIH areas of emphasis potentially relevant to clinical research included topics such as obesity, bariatric surgery, integrative genomics, family health, health disparities, autism, and cancer risk. As your research interests and opportunities evolve, updating your personal NIH timeline and research application strategy might make the path forward clearer.

Each year, over 9,000 competing grant applications are funded NIH-wide. The largest proportion of applications is unsolicited and investigator-initiated. Clinical research is an immense endeavor at NIH and makes up over a third of the entire NIH research grant budget. A cap does not exist on how much NIH will spend on clinical research and the scientific domains receiving NIH clinical research funding are not predetermined. Future support for clinical sleep research at the NIH will be largely determined by the number of grant applications submitted, funds available, and the proportion of these applications identified as highly meritorious by the competitive peer review process. Applicants can anticipate that a strong panel of expert reviewers will be engaged to assess clinical research applications. As applicants, you are in the best position to candidly assess your clinical research plans in terms of focus, clarity, feasibility, "best practices", and team strength for the purpose of NIH competitive peer review. Clinical sleep research also poses specialized challenges including complexity of data collection, burden on study participants, study design, the selection of appropriate outcomes, and interpretation. As domain experts, clinical sleep researchers are also leaders in the process of crisply defining the most compelling study questions for the purpose of competitive peer review. Typically, research objectives will be defined in terms of biology, and not by technological capabilities ("tools").

The chapters that follow highlight many of these questions, best practices and solutions. Dr. Clete Kushida, has brought together useful and informative contributions on many aspects of the application process for scientific research grants. I have had the privilege of following the research of many of the contributors, and they are among the leaders in sleep and sleep medicine research. Their understanding of the application process for the National Institutes of Health (NIH) is evident in their individual histories of NIH-funded research. While some of this information may be specific to sleep-related research, the essence of grantsmanship is universal and can be applied to all areas of science. It is my hope that the readers of this guide will be encouraged to submit grant applications, thereby taking the first steps in launching successful, independent research careers. The discoveries that will result from your individual efforts will help set the pace and momentum of research in the community as a whole.

Michael Twery, PhD
Director, National Center on Sleep Disorders Research
National Heart, Lung, and Blood Institute

Though guide could not exist without the outstanding contributions of the talented group of authors (M. Safwan Badr, Atul Malhotra, Seiji Nishino, Mark R. Opp, Sairam Parthasarathy, Clifford B. Saper, Patrick J. Strollo, Jr., Connie M. Ulrich, Terri Weaver, and Phyllis C. Zee); their detailed and comprehensive works are greatly appreciated. The authors span a wide range of different specialties and interests, including neurology, pulmonary medicine, psychiatry, anesthesiology, nursing, bioethics, and basic and clinical research. The tireless efforts, dedication, and creativity of American Academy of Sleep Medicine (AASM) Executive Director Jerry Barrett and his talented staff were critical in publishing this guide. In addition, Sonia Ancoli-Israel and Naresh Punjabi donated their time in serving as outside reviewers. Lastly, the current AASM Board of Directors (M. Safwan Badr, David R. Bruce, Nancy Collop, Lawrence J. Epstein, Mary Susan Esther, Samuel A. Fleishman, Daniel G. Glaze, Timothy I. Morgenthaler, Steven A. Shea, Patrick J. Strollo, Jr., Nathaniel F. Watson) and Sleep Research Society (SRS) Board of Directors (Sean Drummond, Janet Mullington, Sara Nowakowski, Gina Poe, David Rye, Clifford B. Saper, Thomas Scammell, Ronald Szymusiak, Michael V. Vitiello, James K. Walsh, Terri Weaver, Phyllis C. Zee) were responsible for reviewing and approving the original proposal and the final version of this guide.

I am deeply indebted to a few of the renowned and true pioneers of our field of sleep, William C. Dement, Christian Guilleminault, Sonia Ancoli-Israel, Chris Gillin, and Allan Rechtschaffen, who served as my mentors through various stages of my career. In all of my endeavors, I can always count on my parents, Samiko and Hiroshi Kushida, to assist me; this guide was no exception. This book is dedicated not only to my parents but also to the marvelous team of the Apnea Positive Pressure Long-term Efficacy Study (APPLES), sponsored by the National Heart, Lung, and Blood Institute (NHLBI) of the National Institutes of Health (NIH). I have been very fortunate, along with William C. Dement, to serve as Principal Investigator of APPLES; our team consists of Pamela Hyde, Deborah Nichols, Eileen Leary, Tyson Holmes, Dan Bloch, as well as NHLBI program officials (Michael Twery and Gail Weinmann), site directors, coordinators, consultants, committee members, key Stanford site personnel (Chia-Yu Cardell, Rhonda Wong, Pete Silva, Jennifer Blair), and data and safety monitoring board (DSMB) members.

It is my sincere hope that the reader will use this guide to become an expert in his or her scientific discipline. Available funding for research and the number of young investigators interested in a career in basic or clinical research are areas that need improvement. The interested readers can directly contribute to their fields in several ways: submitting a grant proposal to the National Institutes of Health, applying for membership in scientific or medical societies, serving on committees in these organizations, and/or simply becoming an expert in their area. Lastly, I'll never forget a sticker posted on the door of Mary Carskadon's former office at Stanford that contained words to live by: "Be alert. The world needs more lerts."

Clete A. Kushida, MD, PhD
President, American Academy of Sleep Medicine

CHAPTER I

INTRODUCTION

Clete A. Kushida, MD, PhD

In November 2008, Dr. Michael Twery from the National Heart Lung and Blood Institute (NHLBI) of the National Institutes of Health (NIH) and Dr. Sairam Parthasarathy, chair of the American Academy of Sleep Medicine (AASM) Research Committee discussed creating a collection of core competencies for clinical sleep disorders research for trainees attending the first Young Investigators Forum on sleep-related research. Dr. Parthasarathy asked me to coordinate this effort and submit this request to the AASM Board of Directors. I developed a proposal for a guide focusing on core competencies with expansion on how to develop, write, and implement scientific research grants and presented it to the AASM Board, which approved the plan on January 23-25, 2009. The proposal was also discussed with Dr. Clifford B. Saper, President of the Sleep Research Society (SRS) in February 2009 and approved by the AASM and SRS Executive Committees in February-March 2009.

The Young Investigators Forum was sponsored by the AASM, and was organized by Drs. Richard Berry (Chair), Sai Parthasarathy, M. Safwan Badr, and Steven Shea. It was held on April 15-16, 2009 in the NIH campus in Bethesda, Maryland. With the unflagging support from NIH, especially Dr. Michael Twery, the forum was, by any measure, a tremendous success. One of the goals of this program was to follow the trainees for years after the forum to assess whether the program had prepared the trainees to successfully obtain grants and to effectively launch an academic career. Due to the success of this forum, the program is being continued for as long as the program is able to meet the goals and the expectations of its trainees.

This guide was designed for post-graduate students, residents, fellows, and trainees, but junior faculty should also find it useful. Additionally, PhD students as well as MD students should find relevant and helpful information. The primary focus is NIH-related grants; however, applying for Veterans Affairs, industry, and foundation grants are covered. Although the guide was originally aimed toward those applying for sleep research-related grants, the scope is broad enough that those applying for grants in other disciplines of the basic and clinical sciences will undoubtedly find it useful.

The basic goal of this guide is to encourage individuals to write and submit scientific research grants. Even an individual who has never submitted a grant should find this guide beneficial since it is designed to provide the necessary tools for successful grant writing. The authors were carefully matched to their areas of expertise so that they could provide the best and most relevant advice.

In closing, remember that a grant proposal is not simple to develop, write, and implement, but you will never be awarded a grant if you do not initiate the process—may you be successful in this endeavor!

CHAPTER II

FUNDING SOURCES:
TYPES AND DESCRIPTION

M. Safwan Badr, MD

INTRODUCTION

The rising demand for high quality physician scientists remains unmet as the supply of these scientists has not kept pace. Possible causes include the high cost of recruitment and training of junior faculty, a wide income differential with private practice, the limited pool of qualified physician scientists, as well as the increased complexity of new scientific disciplines. The recruitment, training and retention of clinician scientists are indispensable requirements to advance biomedical research.

Starting an academic career is an exciting and challenging time for the new faculty member. Many feel that building a research career is among their most formidable challenges. There is plethora of general information but a paucity of individualized guidance. The result is uncertainty that defies simple answers and contributes to career anxiety. Another challenge is the difficulty of balancing the multitude of missions in many academic departments. While research is touted as an institutional priority, competing priorities translate to inadequate support for the research careers of junior faculty. Increased competition for faculty time and increased financial challenges has brought these issues to the fore. Finally, obtaining and maintaining competitive extramural research funding has become much more difficult in the past decade. This chapter will discuss the different options available to new investigators as they contemplate how to pursue funding opportunities.

STRATEGIC PLANNING

The hallmarks of successful research careers are: (a) sustained independent funding, (b) high quality peer reviewed publications and (c) mentoring of future scientists. Independent research funding is the corner stone of any successful research career.

Successful competition for research funding requires commitment, dedication, tenacity and a supportive nurturing environment. Therefore, determining career objectives clearly and honestly is the first step before exploring potential research support opportunities. One way to begin the exercise is determine long-term career objectives, using a 10-year point in the future as a milestone. It is important to determine the destination before planning the journey.

Preparing a grant application is a laborious process that takes several months to complete. Therefore, it is critical to confirm that this is the right application for you by understanding the specific requirements, the underlying objectives and the steps required to ensure alignment between your application and the objectives of the funding agency. Funding opportunities for junior faculty provide research support or protected time for highly promising faculty early in their careers. These awards are investments in the careers of budding scientists.

The next step is a critical assessment of the institutional environment for strengths, weaknesses, and opportunities, including a potential network of mentors and collaborators. Identifying an appropriate mentor is one of the most critical elements for career development for junior researchers. A mentor is an advisor, counselor, and friend, guiding the junior faculty through the vicissitudes of career development. An experienced and supportive mentor can also provide the intellectual interaction required for the evaluation of research questions, identification of appropriate funding sources, and the preparation of manuscripts and grant applications.

RESEARCH FELLOWSHIP SUPPORT

A starting scientist who has completed post-graduate clinical training may require additional research training through post-doctoral fellowships. These are available to senior clinical fellows who are committed to future academic careers. Individual fellowships (F32) are available through the National Institutes of Health (NIH). The applications undergo rigorous peer-review and are funded based on overall scientific merit. Criteria for evaluation include the applicant, the research project, the environment and the mentor. Another funding source is through supplemental awards to NIH funded grants, such as the NIH program to provide supplements to support research training for underrepresented minorities. This is a tremendous opportunity for mentorship and scientific growth within an existing successful research program.

Some academic centers may have the ability to hire and support a post-doctoral research associate position. Funding for such a position is derived from existing grants held by a senior scientist or from institutional sources to support a specific research program. A research associate position (or its equivalent) is has a finite term of 2-3 years and provides intensive research training, a dynamic scientific environment and valuable research protected time, leading to an independent research career.

INSTITUTIONAL FUNDING OPPORTUNITIES

The first step for a newly-appointed faculty is to identify institutional career development mechanisms, at the department, school or university level. This would allow the faculty to identify institutional priorities and align their career goals within the institutional framework. While faculty members are free to chart their own independent course, alignment with the institutional goals increases the likelihood of institutional support and enhances the opportunities for mentorship and collaboration. It is also important to identify research related educational offerings at the institution; these may include courses on manuscript preparation, grant writing or biostatistics.

The alignment of goals is critical for career growth. The academic goals and areas of emphasis within a department would determine areas of support and investment. The chances of success are diminished if the faculty member is pursuing an area of investigation that does not fit within the department strategic plans or areas of focus. In contrast, alignment with the department objectives would leverage existing resources and facilitate academic growth. The availability of resources and the criteria for promotion are among the key metrics to determine the viability of a particular path for a new faculty member.

Many departments and schools have established "seed money" funding mechanisms for junior faculty members. The central aim is the promotion of novel high-quality research projects that could lead to extramural grant support. Interestingly, only a small proportion of junior faculty members take advantage of these programs because of the small award size and the effort required. However, the value of engaging the process cannot be measured by the small awarded funds. Instead, seed-money awards provide critical resources to obtain preliminary data that would fortify a subsequent extramural application. Moreover, submitting an application provide an opportunity to understand and refine critical skills related to grant submission and review.

Funding agencies may also provide funds for career development to academic institutions. For example, several, but not all, NIH Institutes and Centers support the K-12 program, which provides support to an institution for career development of independent scientists, with a major focus on physician scientists. It is of note that the National Heart Lung and Blood Institute (NHLBI), National Institute on Aging (NIA) and National Institute of Mental Health (NIMH) do not support this mechanism. Prospective candidates should inquire at their own institution if such an award exists as an option. Other foundations and groups may also provide similar institutional support for junior faculty. The starting point is to inquire through the chain of research administration offices from the department to the university.

EXTRAMURAL FUNDING OPPORTUNITIES

TYPES OF RESEARCH AWARDS

Two broad categories of research awards are available for individual investigators. The first is what is referred to as "Project grants." Examples include grant offered under the R01 mechanism or the MERIT review mechanism in the Department of Veterans Affairs. Such awards fund a specific research project, providing support for equipment, supplies and personnel, including a small salary amount for the salary of the principal investigator (PI). The objective of these awards is to fund the actual research conducted by the investigator. The second type of research awards is the "career development award." The objectives of these awards are to provide mentoring and salary support for protected research time that would allow for career development toward an independent research career. Most of the award funds are dedicated for salary support for the PI, usually around 75% time commitment (not less than 50%). The project support is usually minimal and insufficient to complete the proposed research. However, the mentor or the institution is expected to provide the additional funding required for career development. Examples include the K23 or K08 mechanisms.

SOURCES OF FUNDING

Scientific research can be interdisciplinary, transcending traditional boundaries of specific disciplines to create new scientific knowledge. Funding opportunities exist at many federal agencies and can be accessed on the Internet by searching the following Web site: www.grants.gov. This site is comprehensive but can be overwhelming unless you are searching for a specific program. Within NIH, institutes and centers are the best resources for information on grant opportunities on training programs. For example, the National Center on Sleep Disorders Research (NCSDR), which is housed within the NHLBI of the NIH, is an excellent source for opportunities and areas of focus for sleep research. Likewise, the institutes and centers coordinate the efforts of different groups including federal, public, private and nonprofit groups. Prospective applicants should consult the NIH Web site for information related to research and for guidance and advice on possible opportunities.

The National Institutes of Health provides career development awards through the "K" series. The spectrum of K awards is wide and most are directed at junior faculty or individuals who have completed specialty clinical training and are starting their career as junior faculty members. In addition, the NIH has recently introduced a new career development award offering "Pathway to Independence" awards (K99) to facilitate the transition of junior faculty independent research careers. Two "K" awards stand out as the most common and useful for junior faculty; these are the K23 for research involving human subjects and K08 for research that does not involve human subjects. Other K-series awards are more focused in their scope and requirements and may not be utilized by all NIH institutes. Examples include Career Enhancement Award in Stem Cell Research (K18) or Mentored Quantitative Research Career Development Award (K25). Updated information on these funding opportunities can be found by checking the K Kiosk at The NIH Web site; a "Career Award Wizard" is very helpful to investigators searching for specific information about any of the award opportunities: http://grants1.nih.gov/training/kwizard/index.htm.

The Department of Veterans Affairs (VA) also provides support for biomedical research, including career development awards and project grants. The Research Career Development Program is designed to recruit, train and retain talented VA biomedical researchers in areas of particular importance to VA. There are two levels of career development awards from "CDA 1" as an entry-level award; in contrast, "CDA2" represents a midlevel-program development plan. These are excellent opportunities for VA investigators. To determine eligibility and requirements, it is advisable to review the VA research and development Web site www.research.va.gov.

The National Science Foundation and many foundations and agencies have programs for new investigators. The starting point is to consult the research office at the local institution for advice regarding suitable opportunities. It is important to identify opportunities for junior investigators given the differences in the requirements and selection criteria.

HOW TO ASSESS POTENTIAL OPPORTUNITIES

It is important that applications are aligned to meet the goals of the funding agency and the objectives of the applicant. I recommend a combination of informal discussions with senior colleagues and a meticulous reading of the guidelines and previous funded projects. Informal conversations with senior colleagues can provide valuable career and institutional context. Likewise, I recommend a detailed review of the grant application guidelines to ascertain research priorities and to review previous funding history by the agency to ascertain suitability of your area to the missions and objectives of the agency or grant mechanism. Finally, I would recommend that prospective applicants communicate with a program officer at the organization for advice on the major priorities and about application procedures and current funding priorities.

SUMMARY

Successful competition for research grants is the lifeline of research conducted at academic centers. A targeted, focused approach to seeking grant funding is an essential component of establishing a research career. A career development award, combined with an effective and genuine mentoring program would greatly enhance the likelihood of success in securing research funds and establishing an independent investigative career.

Resources

Brown AM, Morrow JD, Limbird LE, Byrne DW, Gabbe SG, Balser JR, Brown NJ. Centralized oversight of physician-scientist faculty development at Vanderbilt: early outcomes. Academic Medicine 2008;83:969-75.

Chang S, Hughes DC, Chamberlain RM. Works-in-progress: guiding junior scientists through career development applications. J Cancer Educ 2008;23:142-8.

Devine EB. The art of obtaining grants. Am J Health Syst Pharm 2009;66:580-7.

Jacelon CS, Zucker DM, Staccarini JM, Henneman EA. Peer mentoring for tenure-track faculty. J Prof Nurs 2003;19:335-8.

Kupfer DJ, Hyman SE, Schatzberg AF, Pincus HA, Reynolds CF 3rd. Recruiting and retaining future generations of physician scientists in mental health. Arch Gen Psychiatry 2002;59:657-60.

McDonagh KT. Identifying grant funding: mentored career development and transition awards. Hematology Am Soc Hematol Educ Program 2008:12-5.

Nelson JM, Cook PF. Evaluation of a career ladder program in an ambulatory care environment. Nurs Econ 2008;26:353-60.

Perrault C. Grant-writing offices would let scientists get on with research. Nature 2009;458:281.

Puljak L. An overlooked source of physician-scientists. J Investig Med 2007;55:402-5.

Vogler WR. An analysis of the American Cancer Society Clinical Research Training program. J Cancer Educ 2004;19:91-4.

Tudiver F, Ferguson KR, Wilson JL, Kukulka G. Enhancing research in a family medicine program: one institution's story. Fam Med 2008;40:492-9.

Wurmser T, Hedges C. Primer for successful grant writing. AACN Adv Crit Care 2009;20:102-7.

CHAPTER III

MENTORS, COLLABORATORS, AND CONSULTANTS

Sairam Parthasarathy, MD

INTRODUCTION

In his Oscar-worthy performance as the critic Anton Ego in the movie Ratatouille, Peter O'Toole described the critic in all of us and what it means to new entrants into any field of work:

> *"In many ways the work of a critic is easy. We risk very little, yet enjoy a position over those who offer up their work and their selves to our judgment. We thrive on negative criticism which is fun to write and to read. But, the bitter truth that we critics must face is that in the grand scheme of things the average piece of junk is probably more meaningful than our criticism designating itself. But there are times when a critic truly risks something and that is in the discovery and defense of the new. The world is often unkind to new talent, new creations, and new ideas. The new, needs friends."*

The new, needs more than just friends, the new needs mentors. This chapter of the guide will help the reader gain a good understanding of the ideal mentor and mentor-mentee relationship, and what to expect from such a relationship. Moreover, the reader will be advised on some common traps that a beginner faces in research and how to avoid them. Lastly, aspects of how to cobble together various elements of a (mentored) grant—advisory panel, collaborators, consultants, and institutional support—will be discussed. The reader should be aware that the contents of this chapter are just a collection of road signs that are meant to be a guide. They are not to represent a formulaic approach to success nor are they meant to be an authoritarian statement. There are no authorities in science or wisdom, as neither is stagnant: Science is relentlessly corrected by experimentation, and wisdom is continually reshaped by one's experiences. Sharing one's experience, however, can help.

ROLES AND RESPONSIBILITIES OF MENTORS[1]

What are the various roles a mentor takes on? As a **teacher** the mentor imparts technical skills to the mentee that are unique to his or her field of research, and teaches the young investigator how to design studies, conduct research, write, seek funding, and publish. But, such learning cannot be imbibed -- it requires active learning and relearning over the period of apprenticeship which may span many years. Sometimes, a decade or two may pass before the mentee realizes the true and immense value of the teacher's advice. As a **guide**, the mentor helps the mentee take the initial steps to enter the research enterprise. Usually, the mentee latches on to an ongoing research project of the mentor and observes, then participates, and learns. In due time, depending on the progress, the mentor suggests a topic which is usually an extension of the mentor's work, but one that the young investigator can grasp and carry on. Eventually, the mentee embarks on a project which may be quite distinct and original from that of the mentor's own work. Such originality cannot be learned but is an inherent spark and a marker for future promise. At such a time the mentor should sense the need to back off. The honor in mentoring lies in letting the mentees surpass the mentors rather than typecasting them in a mold that resembles their own selves.[2]

As a **protector**, the mentor fends off competing interests that may distract and consume the time of the young investigator.[1] Such competing interests may range from warding off the "bean counters" from the billing and coding department, the buzzards of recruiters for private practice, and to the tantalizing directorships. In a certain sense the mentor applies blinders to the mentee's mind to keep his or her vision focused on the task in front of them, as opposed to being distracted and slowed down. As a **sponsor**, the mentor introduces the young investigator to a new social world in the academic world of research.[1] The mentor may provide access to his or her technicians' time and other facilities and nudges the mentee towards funding sources and other such opportunities. As an **advisor**, the mentor serves as a sounding board and serves to "reality check" new ideas from the young investigator. Depending on the mentor-mentee relationship, the gamut of counsel may not pertain only to professional advice but may span to areas outside the profession. The extent of such a relationship is unique to each mentor-mentee pairing. The mentor also acts as an **agent**[1] – just as do agents of movie stars – the mentor promotes the mentee. When the mentor suggests the mentee as a potential speaker at a conference or symposium the mentee gains much needed exposure in the research community.

Being a **role model**, is an important and heavy burden that a mentor carries.[1] As a role model, the mentor inspires the mentee to be like him or her. However, some role models may not be very approachable. The ideal mentor must be approachable, maintain friendly contact with his mentee, and foster camaraderie amongst his team while being vigilant of where the boundaries lie. Being a **coach** is to know how hard to push while being cognizant of the limits of the mentee. Finally, being a **confidante** is another burden, but also serves as a marker of how strong the mentor-mentee relationship really is. Being available and keeping his or her discussions in strict confidence is a foundation upon which trust is built in this relationship.

MENTOR-MENTEE RELATIONSHIP[2]

Some things are better defined by what they are NOT rather than what they actually are. The mentor-mentee relationship is *not* pure altruism. The mentor stands to gain much in terms of labor, prestige, and interactions with innovative and questioning young minds that spur the mentor's work. Therefore, the relationship is a two-way street.

It is *not* a parent child relationship, although there may be overtones of that. It is *not* an entitlement, as many young investigators may never cross paths with a true mentor. True mentors are a rare commodity. Such a rare commodity, however, may *not* be absolutely necessary. Many preeminent researchers and individuals were never mentored – Einstein and Lincoln to name a few.

Mentor-mentee relationship is *not* a transaction nor should it be seen as favoritism. Such a perception of favoritism may exist outside this relationship, and both the mentor and mentee should be aware of this fact. In the mentor-mentee relationship, there should *not* be an expectation or acceptance of condescension and eternal gratitude, although we see a lot of that. Finally, if anything, it is most certainly *not* stagnant. The relationship evolves over the years until the young investigator grows and matures in stature and they become friends, peers, and colleagues. Some mentors have difficulty with such transition. In such a situation, the mentee should be savvy enough to recognize this shortcoming in the mentor, and should know when to spread wings and fly. But to do so, without hurt feelings, requires much tact.

CHOOSING AND INTERACTING WITH A MENTOR

The modern day young investigator may never exercise true choice in the selection of a mentor. They may be assigned a mentor when they commence the research year of his or her fellowship. But then again, many young investigators may not understand the true meaning of the word mentorship as embodied in the sections above. In a survey of 531 fellows and junior faculty, a large number of "mentors" were identified by participants – an average of 4.6 mentors per respondent.[3] It is unclear if these were role models or mentors in the truest sense of the word as there appeared to be too many mentors so early in their careers. There is some evidence, however, that mentors holding PhD degrees may better organize the mentee's research and career development activities.[3] Such organizational skills were attributed to the mentors' own structured graduate school experiences – graded classes, thesis writing, examinations, defenses, and past experience with advisory committees.[3] Such structure is in stark contrast to the relatively less structured experiences of an MD who proceeds through residency and fellowship. Residents and fellows are like nomads moving month-to-month from one rotation to another. It is truly amazing, and a credit to them when they succeed in their research or clinical endeavors. Nevertheless, there are excellent MD mentors out there, but it would behoove both MD and PhD mentors to adopt a certain structure to their mentorship plan. One such structure to mentoring may lie in clearly identifying mutually agreeable expectations and milestones (**Appendix A**). An additional supplement may be a contract between the mentor, mentee, and the institution (**Appendix B**). Such a contract, however, may not be feasible in all institutions but is a worthy tool to consider.

In the aforementioned study, mentees in pulmonary and critical care reported that their mentors spent more time advising on scientific work rather than career and academic advancement.[3] When choosing a mentor, the young investigator should consider the mentor on the basis of approachability and enthusiasm for mentoring. A prior track record of having successfully mentored individuals who have transitioned into becoming independent investigators can be a reliable indicator. Such a track record is often sought by the National Institutes of Health (NIH) to objectively verify the success rate of a mentor. The mentor's training matrix with information regarding prior mentees, mentees' years of training, degree, type of research, current or last known position and his or her success in securing funding will offer grant reviewers valuable insight (**Appendix C**). If the mentor does not have a prior track record, some granting agencies may consider a co-mentor with such experience. While this may satisfy some granting agencies, this may not be ideal for the mentee's future success. In identifying a potential mentor, the individual's standing in the proposed research area must be solid and they must be currently funded by the granting agency. The mentor's training experience and research occupies top priority in determining the fate of a training grant application.

The mentor should be willing to guide the mentee through the grant application process, provide the required letters of support, and schedule planned interactions with the mentee. In short, the mentor should be willing to invest a significant amount of time and effort in the young investigator. The mentee on the other hand, should recognize this time and effort expenditure. The mentee should keep track of contact time with his or her mentor – emails, face-to-face, during conference and departmental activities, etc. – and give gentle feedback to the mentor if insufficient. The mentee should also seek feedback on his or her performance (especially when it is not forthcoming), and discern the mentor's perception of his or her career trajectory.

On a monthly basis, before interacting with the mentor the mentee should gauge the "season of the year"—is it time to write grants, papers, abstracts, or initiate new projects? The mentee should be cognizant of the fact that there is always a clash of priorities between the mentor and mentee, the least that the mentee can do is to be in sync with the "academic season." If unsure, the mentee should ask and know that knowledge is power.

BEGINNER'S TRAPS[2]

The young investigator should try and avoid the ubiquitous beginner's traps that await him or her. For starters, an **undue admiration of authority** may be detrimental. This usually occurs early in one's research career when they are struck by the "awe factor." They are in awe of their mentors and are unable to see the horizon past the giants in the field. Such feelings may deter some from pursuing research as they compare themselves to their mentor and the mentor's achievements, and incur a feeling a low self-worth. While such modesty may be a virtue, excessive modesty may be detrimental to the beginner's confidence. The mentee should refrain from premature comparisons with the greats, while taking comfort from the fact that a young investigator who achieves a certain degree of success will through his or her discoveries chip away on the achievements of past or contemporary doyens of science.[2]

The sinking feeling that **most important problems are already solved.**[2] Some may end up feeling that there is not much worthwhile left to discover (Alexander exclaimed about the victories of Phillip, "My father is going to leave me nothing to conquer!") The young investigator should persevere in earnest for newer arenas of discovery while standing on the shoulders of giants.

Instrument addiction, a condition this ails young men more than their women peers. Men with their need for gadgets! The author remembers having a "talk" with his mentor. When, faced with explaining lack of productivity, the author found the need for that extra piece of "vital" physiological equipment that would have made the world of a difference in writing productivity. At the mentor's behest, the author became acutely aware that instruments are only the "means" and not the "reasons" for research.

A **perceived lack of ability** is just that, a mere perception. The inability to record a signal, or measure an analyte, may at face value suggest a lack of ability, but may well be worthy of a problem less well understood and become an endeavor of its own right. Vindicating true the adage, "One man's artifact becomes another's signal."

Contemplators contemplate but just can't seem to execute. These are the scientists who have a commitment problem. They should commit to something, "I will have the paper to you by May 1st," and put it in writing. That way they are held accountable. This may be a problem that plagues physician-scientists more than bench researchers. Physician-scientists may find caring for patients as a worthwhile endeavor, and a justifiable excuse to explain their lack of scientific productivity: "I have been saving lives, so, I don't have the time to write that paper yet." This raises the scepter of time management and protected time for research—two nebulous yet crucial areas that can make or break careers. **Poor time management** and **lack of organizational skills** can undermine the most brilliant of minds. For some individuals time management and organization come naturally, but most have to strive hard to manage their time. Taking a break to reorganize one's desk and planner is not wasted time, but "creative procrastination." However, **protected time for research** varies depending on the institution, type of research, mentor, department or section chair, and funding circumstances. The mentee would be wise to trust his or her mentor in navigating through the treacherous waters of institution politics in order to protect his or her time. The mentee should find a mentor that he or she can trust with this complex decision-making process.

Erudite bibliophiles can make a career out of citing other work. Such an encyclopedic knowledge and memory can drain one's energy and take his or her focus away from research. Such memory, however, needs space. If more of the brain were used to store information, then less is available for computation. Such a problem plagues brains too, not just computers.

Megalomaniacs, in this context, are not really the overt raving megalomaniacs who cannot stop talking about themselves. But, these are those who believe that the Curies, Roentgens, and other greats began their careers with their groundbreaking discoveries. They continue to toil away at their "mother of all hypothesis" by plotting, revising, correcting their great work; while there are publications in the same area pouring down and dissolving away at their grandiose plan in bits and pieces.

Being a **theorist** is to have a creative imagination, and an aversion to hard science. "They would rather fashion a beautiful theory than discover a phenomenon."[2]

In sum, it is easier to walk the narrow path to success if one knows where the minefields lie. The above was just the shortlist of such potential minefields. While the above is a list of potential pitfalls and shortcomings, what should be the necessary qualities? Independent judgment, unflagging concentration, a passion for research, an acquired taste for scientific originality, perseverance, perseverance, and some more perseverance are just a few. To this author, it resonated to hear the same word – perseverance – from the mentor, program official, and scientific administrator following an unscored grant proposal.

"WHAT DO YOU WANT?"

What you want may not be what you need. In the aforementioned survey, most young investigators ranked the need for increased visibility as a productive faculty member as their top choice.[3] Other attributes were knowing: (a) how to strike a balance between research and clinical work, (b) requirements for academic promotion, and (c) grant mechanisms in order to advance in their departments. Regrettably, finding and sustaining a mentorship relationship was low on the respondents' collective priority list at 7th of 10 slots. These were the same individuals who reported that they lacked an understanding of their career roadmap and requested greater formal assistance in career development. A good mentor could have assisted with the entire gamut of the mentee's needs.

While guides such as this one can provide a career roadmap the role of a supportive and involved mentor is immeasurable. There are some trainees, however, who feel awkward or afraid to admit openly that they need help. However, Randy Pausch, in his last lecture at Carnegie Mellon summed it by saying, "If you want something bad enough, never give up (and take a boost when offered)."[4]

CAREER DEVELOPMENT PLAN

The initial training grant requires significant input from the mentor. Charting the career development plan is a very important part of both conversations between the mentor and mentee and the writing of the grant application. With the help of the mentor, the young trainee should clearly describe how the grant would support the proposed research work, coursework, and other training opportunities. A training grant (such as a K award) with significant amount of protected time (usually 75%) and a well crafted career development plan can help the mentee transition in becoming an independent investigator. Sample training grants are available at NIH Web sites and serve as an excellent resource.[5] Additionally, mentors and institutions may share previously successful award applications to help the mentee understand the requirements and components of such an application. The application requires writing, proofing, editing, and revising in a perpetual cycle until both the applicant and the mentor are satisfied with the final document. Throughout this process the candidate learns the art of writing. Writing is hard.[6] Writing requires dedication and pursuit for that perfect sentence or section. If the mentee does not envision becoming a professional writer, and enjoying such activity, the pursuit of academia may be in vain. Scientific writing plays an integral role in the dissemination, proper understanding, and even in the conceptualization of science. As in science, in scientific writing, the mentee serves as an apprentice to a master craftsman and in some instances may begin by learning good grammar.[7]

In a training grant application, the candidate's section should transmit his or her passion for research and his or her desire to establish a strong career in academia. The candidate's background should be replete with information of his or her strong background training (clinical and/or bench) and competence while highlighting his or her early research and publication experiences. In training applications, reviewers like to see at least two papers as first author during fellowship, whereas in R01 applications, the reviewers prefer to see much more greater than 10.[8] Prior participation in conferences, peer-review process, and other academic pursuits are a plus.

The trainee should neatly breakdown his or her goals preferably into short-term and long-term goals. While the short-term goals should be crisp, specific, and dovetail nicely with the proposed course work, the long-term goals should emphasize the ultimate career destination as well as be somewhat specific. For example, a short-term goal could be to learn a particular skill set such as how to collect, analyze and interpret a set of data – be it in molecular biology or in clinical epidemiology. The overarching long-term goal would be to develop the skills allowing the applicant to integrate his or her clinical expertise into a clinical research career and to enable him or her to become an accomplished and productive researcher. Whereas, a specific long-term goal would be to identify a safe and effective treatment for condition X. Each section in the training grant should end with a summary to drive home the message in a succinct manner.

The career training activities should clearly itemize what the trainee would be doing at any given point of the award. A nice table or Gantt chart with the planned course works and the projected time should be clearly stated along with the course numbers (**Appendix D**). Each coursework should be briefly described (in a paragraph) to help the reviewer. Other planned training activities such as research seminars, group meetings, guided didactic study with mentors, or attendance at national conferences should also be stated. Additionally, the timeline for the conduct of the research portion of the training grant should be juxtaposed with the Gantt chart that delineates the career development plans so as to show how such work would interdigitate with the proposed course work. Timelines for dissemination of findings (abstracts, presentations, and manuscripts) and application towards independent funding (such as the first R01) should be clearly enunciated. It is very important that the career development plan is "customized" to the trainee and that the plan dovetails with the stated career goals and past experience. Career development plans that appear to contain redundancies with regards to past training experience and proposed course work give the appearance of having being "transplanted" from someone else's grant application, and bode poorly for grant scores. Importantly, clinical/translational research trainees must not fail to clearly describe plans to receive instruction in the responsible conduct of research and protection of human subjects – even if they have had prior experience in the conduct of clinical research.

ADVISORY COMMITTEE

The advisory committee should consist of the mentor, co-mentor (optional), and other senior faculty members. Ideally, the collective expertise of the advisory committee should cover all areas that were proposed in the research plan and career development. A small table listing each member of the advisory committee, their respective roles, and areas of expertise would help the reviewers of the training grant immensely. It is crucial to clearly spell out the frequency (semi-annual or yearly) and method by which the advisory committee would meet and the measures they will use to gauge the progress of the young investigator. A formal mechanism for providing feedback and ensuing action plan should be proposed. A mechanism for resolving conflicts with regards to protected time and competing responsibilities would be a nice touch. This section should provide information regarding the background, stature and accomplishments of each of the advisory committee members. Additionally, the members' biographical sketches and letters committing to advise the candidate should be made available. Both these documents may need certain formatting and required elements to fit the needs of the granting agency. Also, some committee members may be from outside the candidate's institution, in such instances extra emphasis on describing the method and frequency of interactions is expected.

The constitution of this advisory committee must have been established early—at least six months in advance. The support letters must be strong and preferably two-pages long. These letters determine how the applicant is perceived and rated. They should not be disjointed and general, but rather be specific to the application, however, this requires prior coordination. Such coordination could have been achieved by the young investigator when they met with each member of the advisory committee ahead of time regarding the applicant's short- and long-term goals. At that time, the applicant should have shared the specific aims, hypotheses, and rationale of the research plan with the potential advisor. A minimum of 6 months is needed to craft a good proposal. If one were to consider the time taken to collect preliminary data, this would add an additional 6 months to this timeline.

Sometimes, relationships between mentors of the advisory panel and other aspects (such as their time commitments and situations) may change. Having equivalent options for such members of the advisory panel is preferable. Also preferred is a spreadsheet grid of all the requested elements and letters and their respective status. This should become the wallpaper that adorns the mentee's office. Many senior investigators will need reminders, for some it can fluctuate between "You have plenty of time" to "What! You need it in a week!?" with no notice of a middle ground. The applicant would have to pester and persist in order to prevail.

COLLABORATORS AND CONSULTANTS

In general the NIH advises against calling intramural investigators as collaborators. They should be called co-investigators, and ideally they should be paid in proportion to their effort. Both consultants and co-investigators are meant to supplement and enhance the chances of funding rather than to serve as distractions and detract the success of a grant proposal or investigator. Generally, co-investigators are intramural and contribute more effort (and need more salary support) than consultants who are generally extramural. Both consultants and co-investigators should have a strong and current publication track record in the area of required expertise and should be appropriately compensated. An unpaid consultant will dampen enthusiasm with regards to the feasibility of the relationship.[8]

SELECTION PROCESS

When choosing co-investigators and consultants, one should make sure that they bring unique expertise to the proposed research. Redundancies between the co-investigators, consultants, and applicants may raise doubts about the capabilities of the applicant or other members of the team.[8] The selection process sometimes is automatic in a group with prior track record for collaboration. However, it is necessary that there be preliminary discussions and arrangements so as to make sure that everyone is familiar and accepting of their roles, the resources they will commit, and what they will derive from such efforts. More importantly, a prior track record of the investigator working with a co-investigator or consultant will reassure the reviewers that a particular team can indeed work together. This may not be feasible for the young investigator with few publications who is attempting to secure a training grant. In such a situation, the mentor should have established such a prior track record.

Securing strong **letters** of support from consultants and co-investigators is important, but the content of such letters with regards to the final title, addressee, and description of their precise roles, effort percentage, and function are even more important. Unlike letters from the members of the advisory committee, these letters can be one page, but should span at least three-fourths of a page long and be knowledgeable of the contents of the research proposal.[8] Letters with evidence of last-minute receipt, such as being lined by the time and date stamp of the facsimile machine, are to be avoided.

BIOSKETCHES AND OTHER SUPPORT[8]

The **biosketches** from collaborators and co-investigators should be current. Biosketches e-mailed by secretaries and assistants may be outdated, or worse, contain inaccuracies with regards to current funding. These documents change constantly, and outdated biosketches may cast aspersions on whether a relationship is current and viable. However, there are very few investigators who constantly update their electronic versions of their biosketches. Therefore, the investigator should give them adequate forewarning that a letter and updated biosketch would be needed over the next few weeks or month. These biosketches are evidentiary of the extent of collaborative work between the proposed team members. Special emphasis should be given to select and showcase manuscripts and research grants that are common to both the applicant and the collaborators and those that emphasize the needed expertise of a particular consultant. For example, a preeminent researcher in cancer may have worked on both the molecular biology of lung and colon cancer. If the application focuses on lung cancer, then the publications on lung cancer should be preferentially selected while maintaining the appearance of adequate current productivity.

To help out the grant reviewer, the name of the investigator should be depicted in bold font in the publications so that they can quickly discern the number of first authored papers. The quality of the journals matters, but author position and current productivity matter even more. A sample biosketch is provided at the end of this chapter **(Appendix E)**. Ideally the first 2 pages should house the publications and the last 2 pages of the biosketch should house current and completed support over the previous 3 years. Lack of length of biosketch occupied by publications can raise serious concerns. One should not "pad" the publications with abstracts, presentations, and book chapters. The applicant should exercise choice in editing out case reports and letters to the editor if there are too many of them, and always list the publications in chronological order. Inclusion of PubMed Central (PMC) reference number (e.g., PMCID234567) for each article, or if the PMCID is not yet available, indicating that "PMC Journal is in Process" is desirable. If applicable, for manuscripts that derived from NIH funding support, the NIH Manuscript Submission reference number (e.g., NIHMS97531) should be listed. Citations that are publicly available in a free online format may include Uniform Resource Allocator (URL; also known as *Web Address*). Inclusion of manuscripts that have been submitted or are in preparation are to be avoided at all costs.

For the honors section, one should be very selective. This is tough to edit! Editorial positions, assignment to review sections, local and national awards, chairmanship of reputable national or international societies are deserving of mention. The applicant should refrain from itemizing society memberships, board certifications, ad hoc reviewer assignments for journals, and traineeships in this section. Although receipt of trainee travel awards may be considered a plus when applying for a training (K) award.

Care should be taken to accurately fill out the "Research Support" section of the biosketch. Inaccuracies in this section may unfavorably impact the evaluation of one's grant application. Existing grant support that is relevant to the research proposed should be listed first. However, the 2-3 lines describing the overall goal should clearly distinguish the funded work form the proposal under consideration. The applicant should not confuse the research support section of the biosketch with the "Other support" information. While the overall goals of the projects and the responsibilities of the applicant should be identified in the biographical sketch, the number of person months or direct costs should not be listed in the biosketch.

Other support information is requested after peer review, and before the grant is awarded, for NIH staff to ascertain whether the proposed research is not already funded by other funding agencies. The proposal that is under consideration should not be listed under "other support" section. The presence or absence of overlap should be explicitly stated. In the event of overlap, the applicant should indicate how this would be resolved. An example, would be, "There is scientific overlap between the VA Merit Review and the R01 application under consideration. If both are funded, then the VA Merit Review will be surrendered and the NIH R01 will be retained." Lastly, there is a tendency to not call small "start up" funds for what they are. Such grants may not only fail to strengthen the proposal, but may give an appearance of wealth and negatively impact the chances of funding. Consider calling these grants – "start up" funds.

Some well funded co-investigators may appear to be overcommitted. This applies to individuals with certain roles such as statisticians, who may be on multiple funded proposals for 1.2 calendar months each. A careful explanation of this individual's function may be needed to avoid the reviewers' perception that the individual may be over committed. Alternatively, an extremely accomplished and well funded co-investigator may truly be over-committed. Careful consideration of the investigator's role, strengths, and further minimizing percentage effort need to be undertaken before considering an alternate.

INSTITUTIONAL AND DEPARTMENTAL SUPPORT

"Viewed from the summit of reason, all life looks like a malignant disease and the world like a madhouse." Johann Wolfgang von Goethe (1749 - 1832)

Yes. Sometimes, it may seem like a mad house full of individuals with malignant intent and no ability to reason. As the young investigator tries to seek protected time, resources, and institutional and department chair letters for his or her training grant, he or she may get disillusioned. They may struggle, or worse, fail, to get that magic threshold percentage of protected research time or that vital letter of agreement between two parent institutions or departments. The competition is tough, and the resources are scarce. This is when having a powerful mentor, or a mentor with excellent skills in conflict resolution, can help tremendously. In many institutions, such roadblocks are common place.

A training grant requires a lot of support from the institution. Besides the required percentage of protected research time preceding the initiation of the grant (ideally 75% for a K award), the institution should maintain this commitment in the strictest sense following the start of the funding period. For clinical researchers, the clinic times or important division or department meetings could conflict with course times. Some courses offer the flexibility of catching up online through webcast of the classes and homework. The young trainee should explore these options to resolve such time conflicts. Institutions with resident K30 (clinical research training) programs or CTSA have been guaranteed strong commitments by various departments, and trainees in such institutions usually have a well trodden path. However, trainees from smaller institutions have a much harder time. Even in institutions with K30s, the pathway to obtain a Master's degree versus a training certificate or PhD may be varied and unclear. The young trainee needs to spend time asking the right questions to the right people to figure out these pathways and identify the best fit. For clinical researchers, this may be the only time they will be able to enhance their "tool box." Re-tooling later on in their career can take a tremendous amount of effort. Institutions with a prior track record of jostling individuals through this pipeline do a better job of pointing new trainees in the right direction. This is the reason why funding agencies weigh institutional environment into the score of a training grant application.

How much time do you need to get your training grant? It is vital that this be determined prior to a clinical researcher accepting a position. When the trainee has negotiated and accepted a job position, the percentage of protected research time and the duration of such support are vital. Having 75% of protected time for a 3 year period would be golden. But, this is usually not feasible. A two year period of 75% protection with some seed money and a solid mentor is an excellent package. Eighteen month time frame is needed in order for a trainee to apply, and revise and reapply, before a K award funding can start. That is if everything goes smoothly. An extra 6 month period is desirable. Some institutions prefer that a fellow stay on as a senior research (fourth) year fellow and secure his or her K-award, before they can become eligible for securing a faculty position. Some divisions may not have even a single individual without a K or R01 award. The young investigator should wonder whether this is because they are all so very successful, or because unfunded individuals are ruthlessly eliminated, and funding is a pre-requisite to gain entry. Such standards are set by the leadership at the division, department, or institutional level. The young investigator should ask questions and inquire about the local culture before signing on. More importantly, the young investigator should critically review the clinical or teaching commitments against the protected time with the help of an unbiased senior investigator (preferably mentor). The candidate has to remember, that most institutions are juggernauts, and are less caring about the individual when it comes to the institutional priorities and budgets. However, the individuals that work within these institutions are more caring and cognizant of how certain unfavorable decisions can impact a young trainee. It is these compassionate and worthy individuals that the young candidate needs to seek and find. The young trainee is faced with many obstacles, and institutions, even ivory towers, are built with brick walls. But, as Randy Pausch said in his last lecture, "Brick walls are there for a reason. And once you get over them – even if someone has practically had to throw you over – it can be helpful to others to tell them how you did it."[4] Hopefully the reader lands softly in a good place in life, but when you are successful, remember to light the way for others.

ACKNOWLEDGEMENTS

My sincere thanks to my mentors, Drs. Stuart Quan and Martin Tobin, and to many others who helped me get over brick walls. Funding support during time of writing this chapter: NIH/NHLBI 1R01HL095748.

REFERENCES

1.   Tobin MJ. Mentoring: seven roles and some specifics. Am J Respir Crit Care Med 2004;170:114-7.

2.   Advice for a young investigator. S. Ramon Y Cajal; translated by Swanson N and Swanson LW. MIT Press;1999.

3.   Weinert CR, Billings J, Ryan R, Ingbar DH. Academic and career development of pulmonary and critical care physician-scientists. Am J Respir Crit Care Med 2006;173:23-31.

4.   Pausch R, Zaslow J. The Last Lecture. New York: Hyperion; 2008.

5.   http://www.nhlbi.nih.gov/funding/training/redbook/k23models.htm [last accessed August 9, 2009]

6.   Zinsser W. On writing well. New York: Harper Collins; 2006.

7.   Strunk Jr W., White EB. The elements of style – 4th ed. New York: Longman; 2000.

8.   Ogden TE, Goldberg IA. Research proposals. A guide to success. San Diego: Academic Press; 2002.

Appendix A Progress in Career Development Plan [Courtesy Dr. Susan Redline]

Goal: Become a productive researcher				
Objectives	Educational/Training Activity	Research Activity	Product/Dates	Current Status/Progress

Goal: Become a…				
Objectives	Educational/Training Activity	Research Activity	Product/Dates	Current Status/Progress

Goal: Become an effective research team member providing…				
Objectives	Educational/Training Activity	Research Activity	Product/Dates	Current Status/Progress

Sairam Parthasarathy, MD

Appendix B Mentorship Contract [Courtesy Dr. Susan Redline]

Confidentiality – Mentor and Mentee acknowledge that personal and professional confidences will be treated as such and that the parties will endeavor to maintain a relationship built on mutual trust and respect.

Frequency of Meetings – Parties agree to regular meetings. At least one face-to-face meeting a week with the mentor is desirable, but all meetings are dependent upon the individual and the mentee's needs. At least biannual meetings are to be held with the mentor and mentee. Meeting schedules should be defined by the participants.

Mentor's Primary Objectives/Expectations – Parties articulate what each hopes to extract from the relationship. The mentee defines what personal/professional goals h/she hopes to achieve. These are reviewed regularly (minimally at each biannual meeting). Mentees are expected to assume an active, self-directed involvement in their own development.

Roles – The Mentor and Mentee each agree on specific roles. The Mentor is expected to be a teacher, advisor, counselor, role model, guide, and communicator. The Mentee is expected to participate as a learner, absorber, informer, emulator, performer, and communicator.

Progress Reporting – The Mentor and mentee agree on review of regular progress reports and actions plans (at least biannually.)

Success Criteria – All parties agree on how a successful mentoring relationship will be defined. All partied agree to handle potential failure to meet expectations or conflicts as outlined under Institution's Mentoring Guidelines.

Duration – The duration of the mentor program is 6 months for each pairing with a "no-fault" provision for either who desires to discontinue participation at any time. After the sponsorship, pairings may continue their relationship informally.

The Program Director of the research training program will act as liaison between the Mentor/Mentee pairings. The Program Director will also act as a resource to participants and assist in resolving problems/conflicts. The Program Director will be held to the same standard of confidentiality as that expected of the Mentors/Mentees.

We are entering into a voluntary Mentoring relationship that we expect will be mutually beneficial. We want this to be a rich, rewarding experience with most of our time spent in substantive developmental activities. To minimize confusion, frustration, and administrative details, we have noted the following features of our relationships:

Confidentiality: _____

Frequency of Meetings:
   With Mentor: _____

   With Mentor/Program Director: _____

   With Program Director alone: _____

Role of Mentor: _____

Role of Program Director: _____

Role of Co-mentor: _____

Progress Report Frequency: _____

Success Criteria: _____

Duration of Relationship: _____

Resolution of Conflicts: _____

_____   _____
Mentee   Date

_____   _____
Primary Mentor   Date

_____   _____
Program Director   Date

Appendix C Mentor's Training Matrix

Name of Mentor	Trainees (Status while in Training)	Training Period	Degree	Title of Research Project while Training with this Mentor	Current or Last Known Position	Current or last known research type and topic; Sources of Support
John Smith, MD	Doe, Jane Post-doc	1992-1994	University of Antarctica (1984) MD	Circadian Rhythm in the South Pole	Professor, University of Antarctica	Effect of Global Warming on Circadian Rhythm
	Holliday, Doc fellow	1993-1999	University of Tombstone (1987)	Prevalence of Sleep Apnea in Cowboys	Associate Professor, University of Tombstone	Sleep Disorders in Southwestern Drifters

Sairam Parthasarathy, MD

Appendix D Career Development Activities

Career Development Activities	Years				
	1	2	3	4	5
Formal Courses					
Biostatistics	✓				
Introduction to Public Health Statistics (course #)	✓				
Biostatistics in Public Health: Section 1 & 2 (course #)	✓				
Biostatistics in Public Health: Section 3 & 4 (course #)	✓				
Biostatistics for Research: Section 1 (course #)	✓				
Basic Principles of Epidemiology (course #)	✓				
Epidemiological methods (course #)	✓				
Bioethics, Regulations, and Repercussions in Research (course #)	✓				
Design and Analysis of Clinical Trials (course #)		✓			
Grantsmanship (course #)	✓				
Advanced methods in biostatistics (course #)		✓			
Training: Depression screening; Evaluation of PTSD symptoms	✓				
Guided Didactic Study with Mentors	✓	✓	✓	✓	✓
Research Seminars					
University of Timbuktu Clinical Research Training Program	✓	✓	✓	✓	✓
Sleep Medicine Grand Rounds	✓	✓	✓	✓	✓
Department of Neurology, Research Lecture Series	✓	✓	✓	✓	✓
Department of Medicine, Research Seminars	✓	✓	✓	✓	✓
Sleep Disorder Center Weekly Meetings	✓	✓	✓	✓	✓
National Meetings: APSS international meetings, American Thoracic Society	✓	✓	✓	✓	✓
Mentors/Consultants:					
– Primary Sponsor	✓	✓	✓	✓	✓
– Co-sponsor	✓	✓	✓	✓	✓
– Advisor	✓	✓	✓	✓	✓
– Advisor	✓	✓	✓	✓	✓
– Advisor	✓	✓	✓	✓	✓
K23/K08 research plan					
Hire and train research assistant	✓				
Hire and train part-time Sleep technician	✓				
Project organization	✓	✓			
Screen and recruit eligible patients		✓	✓	✓	
Efficacy and safety trial		✓	✓		
Data entry and management		✓	✓	✓	
Data analysis			✓	✓	✓
Manuscript submission					✓
Dissemination: ATS and APSS meetings; Publications				✓	✓
RO1 grant					
Prepare RO1 grant and submit				✓	
Revise, if necessary, and resubmit					✓

Appendix E Sample Biosketch

BIOGRAPHICAL SKETCH

Provide the following information for the Senior/key personnel and other significant contributors.
Follow this format for each person. **DO NOT EXCEED FOUR PAGES.**

NAME	POSITION TITLE
eRA COMMONS USER NAME *(credential, e.g., agency login)*	

EDUCATION/TRAINING *(Begin with baccalaureate or other initial professional education, such as nursing, include postdoctoral training and residency training if applicable.)*

INSTITUTION AND LOCATION	DEGREE *(if applicable)*	MM/YY	FIELD OF STUDY

A. **Personal Statement.** Briefly describe why your experience and qualifications make you particularly well-suited for your role (e.g., PD/PI, mentor) in the project that is the subject of the application.

B. **Positions and Honors.** List in chronological order previous positions, concluding with your present position. List any honors. Include present membership on any Federal Government public advisory committee.

C. **Peer-reviewed publications or manuscripts in press (in chronological order).** NIH encourages applicants to limit the list of selected peer-reviewed publications or manuscripts in press to no more than 15. Do not include manuscripts submitted or in preparation. The individual may choose to include selected publications based on recency, importance to the field, and/or relevance to the proposed research. When citing articles that fall under the Public Access Policy, were authored or co-authored by the applicant and arose from NIH support, provide the NIH Manuscript Submission reference number (e.g., NIHMS97531) or the Pubmed Central (PMC) reference number (e.g., PMCID234567) for each article. If the PMCID is not yet available because the Journal submits articles directly to PMC on behalf of their authors, indicate "PMC Journal – In Process." A list of these journals is posted at: http://publicaccess.nih.gov/ submit_process_journals.htm. Citations that are not covered by the Public Access Policy, but are publicly available in a free, online format may include URLs or PMCID numbers along with the full reference (note that copies of publicly available publications are not acceptable as appendix material).

D. **Research Support.** List both selected ongoing and completed (during the last three years) research projects (Federal or non-Federal support). Begin with the projects that are most relevant to the research proposed in this application. Briefly indicate the overall goals of the projects and responsibilities of the Senior/Key Person identified on the Biographical Sketch. *Do not include number of person months or direct costs.*

Adapted from: http://grants.nih.gov/grants/funding/424/SF424_RR_Guide_General_Adobe_VerB.doc

CHAPTER IV

SELECTING THE RESEARCH QUESTION

Atul Malhotra, MD and Patrick J. Strollo, Jr., MD

BEFORE YOU START

There are a number of considerations to make before investing the time and effort into a grant application.

Select a question/hypothesis which you find exciting. There is nothing more tedious than spending countless hours reading and writing about a topic which you don't find inspiring.

Make sure your question can feasibly be answered. A common mistake is to take on too much or to try to answer a question which cannot be reasonably addressed within the allotted time. Having a long term plan is to be encouraged but if your ideas come across as grandiose, the reviewers will not take you seriously.

Select an appropriate granting mechanism. Explore online which type of grant would be most appropriate for you. Talk to your colleagues and supervisors about what type of grant would be feasible for you to get. For example, some granting mechanisms have been historically receptive to sleep applications, whereas others seem to lack interest. While you should also be thinking about new granting mechanisms, you are probably best off sticking with mechanisms in which your mentor has a track record with prior trainees. Many universities have a Red Book or an online source for available grant mechanisms.

Select the right mentor/environment. There are a variety of factors that go into these decisions including social as well as scientific ones. Your probability of getting funded as a junior person is lower if your mentor does not have funding or a strong scientific reputation. Selecting a very junior mentor may be good from standpoint of camaraderie and communication/social interaction; however, including established senior scientists can give your grant credibility. Be comfortable with your relationship with your mentor. You will be spending a considerable amount of time with him/her. If you do not have the right chemistry in the relationship, you should reconsider moving forward in the process. The mentor you choose should be comfortable enough with their career that he/she is willing and able to create independent opportunities for you and promote your science. Consider including investigators from outside institutions since the NIH and other granting agencies are encouraging these types of collaborations. Remote mentorship programs have been successful in the field of sleep. Consider using the NIH CRISP (Computer Retrieval of Information on Scientific Projects) search on-line to identify potential experts in your field both within your institution and outside. If you can identify mentors with grants listed on CRISP, this will help your chances of being funded.

Look at old grants with a similar funding mechanism. If you decide you should apply for a National Research Service Award (NRSA), find individuals who have successfully competed for an NRSA and ask if they will share with you. Many mentors and trainees are willing to share old grants, particularly if you promise to keep the science confidential. There are some "model" grants that are available online which you can find with Google searches. If you read prior grants, it will give you a better sense of what your task will involve.

Read the instructions. Most grants will give detailed instructions regarding the format or what they are seeking. Failure to follow these instructions can give the reviewers a poor impression and in some cases, the grant may be administratively withdrawn (without ever reaching the reviewers).

GENERAL POINTS

There are a few general principles which you should consider as you put together your grant.

Grants should be as close to perfect as possible. Applicants should be mindful of typographical and grammatical errors before submitting a final version. One anonymous reviewer was heard making the statement, "If this is how he treats his grants, I wonder how he treats his data." Even issues with formatting, etc. are important for grants and should be optimized to the best of your ability. If you are not good with graphics or word-processing, ask friends for help so you can improve your application.

Remember that a grant is not a contract. You may choose to include information in your application for "grantsmanship" which may or may not be in your eventual plans. You never want to be dishonest, but there are times that reviewers will be looking for certain details that you may or may not wish to pursue.

A grant is not copyrighted. If you have written a prior grant on a similar topic, there is no harm in cutting and pasting relevant portions of the grant. This is not duplicate publication or plagiarism. You can also take portions of grants from your collaborators (with permission) as long as you are not representing someone else's work as your own. However, it is important to ensure the "copy-and-pasted" material is stylistically similar to the other text in the grant application.

Many junior grants are too ambitious. While we all have a tendency to want to "do everything," this approach fares poorly with reviewers. Remember the KISS (Keep It Simple Stupid) principle. Even if you know you can answer many different questions with the grant, the reviewer wants to see clear and simple questions that you can answer.

Think about the grant from the reviewer's perspective. Avoid long blocks of text. If you can include figures or tables it helps to break the monotony that can occur when reviewers are reading piles of grants preparing for a study section. Nobody appreciates having to read excessive amounts of materials (e.g., in an appendix or supplemental information). Using excessively small fonts or narrow margins can antagonize reviewers and, in some cases, can lead to administrative withdrawal of the grant. Make the figures big and the legends legible. You are better off making a few points well rather than trying to tell the reviewer everything you know.

Think carefully about what literature to cite. If you know who the reviewers are likely to be, you should consider citing their relevant work. Excessively citing your own work or that of your mentor may antagonize reviewers.

Consider the use of underlining. While clearly excessive underlining is ineffective, the occasional use to emphasize important points can be quite effective. The reviewers are generally drawn to such areas. Casual readers of the grant (e.g., members of the review panel who are not assigned your grant but still involved in scoring) may only read the emphasized portions. Some strong grants will underline roughly one sentence or phrase on each page of the grant to emphasize the most important information on each page. Some amount of repetition can also help to capture the most critical points.

Budget enough time to accomplish your task. This insures thoughtful review by your mentor(s) and ample opportunity to incorporate recommended changes. Seasoned grant writers generally will spend at least 100 hours on a grant submission. If you are writing your first grant expect to invest more time. Most universities require internal review by departmental research committees as a way of providing additional quality control and peer review prior to submitting the application to the funding agency. There is frequently a built in time delay for the office of research to "process the grant" and review the budget prior to submission. This process may take up to one month depending on the institution and is usually non-negotiable for junior investigators.

SELECTING THE OUTCOMES AND SPECIFIC AIMS

A commonly cited statistic is that 50 percent of grants are made or lost on the Specific Aims. This statistic is hard to validate, but the reality is that if the reviewer is not excited about your application by the time he/she has finished reading your Specific Aims, you have likely lost the battle.

Think carefully about how the grant should start. You only get one chance to make a first impression. Consider using a figure or diagram or a quote from a patient to grab the reader's interest.

The reviewer wants to see focused hypotheses. Aims that are too broad or descriptive usually fare poorly. Grants with no hypotheses seldom do well. If an analysis is exploratory, be very clear to label it as such. You can often define a primary outcome measure and label the remainder of your outcomes as exploratory, rather than running what reviewers refer to as a "fishing trip." See **Table 1** for examples of poor aims and how they can be improved.

Table 1 Specific Aims

Examples of Poor Aims	How to Fix
To describe the pattern of cytokines seen with sleep deprivation	To test the hypothesis that IL6 levels are increasing following 36 hours of sleep deprivation
To determine risk factors for obstructive sleep apnea in a certain cohort	To test the hypothesis that neck circumference is an independent predictor of obstructive sleep apnea in cohort X.
To define the important neurotransmitters in the brainstem	To define the impact of 5HT2a at the hypoglossal motor nucleus

Avoid self-predicated aims. If one of your aims fails, the remaining aims should still be fundamentally interesting and important. Many grants turn into a "house of cards" if the application is predicated on one experiment showing what you think it might.

Strong preliminary data can help sell specific aims. If you are reasonably confident that you can prove your stated hypotheses, the reviewer will be able to recognize this. However, avoid overconfidence since you need to make it clear that you have considered alternative hypotheses. Thus, read your specific aims with your preliminary data in mind, knowing that the reviewer will be skeptical about aims that you cannot support.

Once you have written your aims, you should distribute them to colleagues for feedback and critique. If you send a completed grant to colleagues, you need to recognize that this is a considerable amount of work for them to provide useful critique. On the other hand, distributing your Specific Aims can be fairly easy for others to review. If you make substantial revisions to your Aims based on this feedback, you will have saved a considerable amount of time having to re-write other portions of the grant. For example, after your revision, if you decide to exclude brain imaging from your Aims, then you do not need Background and Methods related to imaging.

Literature Review

Doing a literature review is important. However, you do not necessarily need to perform an exhaustive literature review to convince reviewers that you know the literature. Some junior investigators will spend countless hours doing background reading (which is clearly important in science and for your general understanding of the field), but can take over from the focus on the grant application.

Provide synthesis. Listing off a series of papers with conclusions from each abstract does not require an understanding of the science. You are better off making statements which summarize the literature and put it into context. For example, charts and tables which summarize the literature can be appealing to reviewers. Another example might be statements like, "The bulk of the literature showing negative results have used a low dose of drug x as compared to the positive studies."

When you do review the literature, make sure the reviewer keeps your Aims in mind. As you review published papers it is useful to refer back to the questions you plan to answer. For example, if you are studying gender differences in apnea consequences, you should review the literature on apnea consequences but emphasize which major papers did not include adequate numbers of women. Making a table of the relevant papers and listing the numbers of women in each of the relevant papers will emphasize your point further.

Draw conclusions from the literature. Reciting abstracts is not helpful in general. At the end of your Background and Significance, provide a Summary of the Relevant Literature, but include deficiencies which are not resolved but which you plan to address. Remember that the reviewers may have been authors of prior literature so avoid being overly harsh if not necessary. For example, rather than saying, "The literature showing obesity causes fatigue has ignored OSA," consider the statement, "Prior literature linking obesity with fatigue has raised interesting questions regarding the potential causal role of OSA in mediating this association." If your literature summary showcases the need for your proposed experiments, this will appeal to reviewers.

PRELIMINARY DATA

As a junior investigator, having strong preliminary data can help distinguish you from other applicants. If you have minimal data that are relevant, consider postponing the application until such data are available.

After each section, consider making points to the reviewer. For example, the statement, "These data illustrate the feasibility of the proposed research, the potential importance of Neuropeptide Y and the applicant's ability to make the planned measurements." If you need to include preliminary data that are not directly relevant to your application, make sure to highlight what you want the reviewers to learn from it. For example, "These data illustrate the applicant's commitment to academics and long standing interest in neurobiology." Another example would be, "These data illustrate the applicant's knowledge of statistics which will likely be helpful in the analyses of the present application."

Find the right balance of too much vs. too little preliminary data. Inadequate preliminary data can make the reviewer lose confidence. On the other hand, excessive preliminary data could make your proposed experiments seem redundant. Ideally, you show strong trends but without statistical significance and emphasize the need for further work and lack of power to draw definitive conclusions.

If you have no preliminary data for a particular Aim, consider showing a figure to illustrate feasibility. For example, even if you have never done upper airway imaging, you could likely acquire images from a radiology collaborator (or even on yourself) and show that you can measure important variables. Rather than saying in words that you only have n = 1, you can show the image and state "These data illustrate the applicant's ability to acquire the data and perform the necessary analyses." If you are performing an intervention, you could show example data from before and after the intervention rather than emphasizing that you have minimal data. You could then state in a Figure Legend – "Note the change in Parameter X after the intervention compared to baseline." Such illustrative figures can be helpful to showcase important trends even when preliminary data are sparse.

ANALYSES

Although methodological details are important, many junior investigators provide excessive information that uses up precious space. In many cases, if the methods of the laboratory are well established, they can be largely cited in the existing literature. You are better off using the space to give details of your specific protocol or planned experiments. Consider adding a table/figure that illustrates the sequence of data collection related to the protocol – this is of particular help in human investigations in which many data elements are collected (i.e., questionnaires, biomarkers, physiologic signals, etc.). As mentioned above, this strategy helps communicate your point visually and decreases reviewer fatigue.

Don't shortchange the statistics section. Some reviewers will focus primarily on this section since this may be the section that they understand best. Consider including a statistician in your application, but do not assume that this will alleviate all statistical concerns. Provide rigorous power calculations (including means, standard deviations, alpha, beta, etc.) so the reviewers can duplicate your calculations if need be.

Include a section on data synthesis and interpretation. This section can help to convince the reviewers that you have considered all possibilities and you are not assuming you know the results. The section also gives you the chance to show how you can think logically and plan subsequent experiments regardless of the results. For example, if you have follow-up experiments planned regardless of the results of your study, this will impress the reviewers. If Treatment A is better than standard of care control group, then a multicenter trial should be considered. If Treatment A is inferior to standard of care control group, then we will pursue Treatment C. If treatment A is equal to the standard of care control group, we will then consider two possibilities. First, the study may have been underpowered and we can consider further research depending on statistical considerations. Second, the two treatments may really be equivalent. If the treatments are equivalent, we can then plan experiments to define subgroups of patients who may benefit from Treatment A (based on genetic or other biomarkers) or patients in whom Treatment A may be more cost effective.

Consider a table for your various outcome measures. Make crystal clear which are your primary outcome measures (that for which you are powered to show a difference) and which ones are secondary. Making this table can help you organize your thoughts, but will also show the reviewer that you have a clear analytical plan. Such an approach can be much more effective than simply stating "We will examine which polysomnographic variables predict our primary outcome."

Avoid multiple comparisons. Exploratory research has an important role, but studying large panels of cytokines with no clear hypothesis is frowned upon. Your table of outcome measures will help reassure the reviewers that you are not simply "fishing" for positive results.

OTHER SECTIONS OF THE GRANT PROPOSAL

Consider including a timetable towards the end of the grant. This timetable can help give the reviewers confidence that the proposed experiments can and will be accomplished. Include coursework and administrative tasks on the timetable as well as subsequent grant applications. Include summary statements to help convince the reviewers that you have thought about the road to success. Excessive courses or meetings can be a distraction from the laboratory so the timetable can be used to illustrate how much time you will have to focus on the science.

A section on Future Directions can also be helpful. This section can help convince the reviewers that your research may ultimately have a major impact on biomedical research. For example, "If treatment A shows promise, we can then design multicenter randomized trials which may ultimately change standard of care". This section can also help to convince reviewers that you are planning more than descriptive research. For example, "If our hypotheses are indeed confirmed in the present application, we will then be in an excellent position to pursue underlying mechanism" or "Depending on the results of the proposed research, we may develop an animal model to test the mechanism underlying phenomenon X."

A section on Potential Pitfalls can be helpful to alleviate reviewer's concerns. By acknowledging that you realize the limitations in your techniques, you can be less susceptible to critique. You obviously do not want to highlight any fatal flaws, but rather you want to reviewers to know that if your studies fail, you will be in a position to design subsequent studies. No research protocol is perfect, so your acknowledgement can go a long way. For example, consider the statement, "We recognize that we are underpowered to show any improvements in mortality (a secondary outcome), but believe that the proposed research should be completed before the expense and risk of a larger trial can be justified."

FINAL THOUGHTS

Have a thick skin. Remember most grants are rejected, so do not get discouraged regardless of the outcome of your grant. Overly harsh comments from reviewers frequently reflect issues with the reviewer or issues the reviewer has with your mentor rather than you. Remember that even if the payline is 20 percent, this number does not mean that 80 percent of people fail. The 20 percent figure reflects the percentage of applications funded for a submission cycle, but does not consider that you can apply for multiple different funding mechanisms (K23, K08, K99, Fellow-to-Faculty awards) through various different agencies. Even if you are rejected on the first submission, you can usually reapply. The new NIH guidelines, allow only one rather than the previous two re-submissions so it is extremely important to address the critique as fully as possible. Thus, the cumulative percentage for success is much higher than the paylines might imply.

Read the critiques carefully and show them to others. There is a natural tendency to read the critiques immediately after receiving the unsuccessful score. If you go back and re-read the critiques several times you will get a much better sense of whether the reviewers think your grant is "fixable" or whether it is hopeless. Even seemingly hopeless grants can frequently be refocused or revised and sent to a different funding agency with very different results.

Have fun. Creating new knowledge as an investigator should be stimulating and rewarding. For the physician scientist, the research experience may not have a payoff that is as immediate as in patient care, but the excitement and satisfaction of moving the field forward resonates deeply for many of us. The benefits of the experiences and friendships related to scientific collaboration can be immeasurable.

CHAPTER V

STUDY DESIGN FOR HUMAN STUDIES

Terri Weaver, PhD and Connie M. Ulrich, PhD

INTRODUCTION

Research design is the roadmap or blueprint for developing and conducting the research study. It designates the method by which you answer research questions and test your hypotheses. One of the goals of research design is to reduce the sources of extraneous error leaving the variance associated with the effect of the independent variable on the dependent variable. But in reality, there are often other sources of variance in experiments conducted in humans. Your objective in designing your study is to reduce those sources of error. In other words, if you think about the total variance in an experiment, as a pie chart, you want to reduce that proportion that does not relate to the primary associations examined in the study. There are two types of empirical designs – non-experimental or observational and experimental. Non-experimental designs include qualitative, survey, and correlational design categories and the rubric of experimental designs encompasses quasi-experimental studies as well as the gold standard randomized controlled clinical trial. We will restrict the discussion in this chapter to quantitative research methods.

THREATS TO VALIDITY

The selection of a research design takes into consideration the threats to validity that may compromise the quality and generalizability of the data and the desire to control these factors. There are several types of validity: statistical conclusion validity, internal validity, construct validity, and external validity.

Statistical conclusion validity reflects the validity of the assumptions about the correlation (covariation) between treatment and outcome. This consideration comes into play with the determination of sample size (discussed below). Threats to statistical conclusion validity occur when there is an inadequate sample size relative to the statistical test employed leading to low statistical power, and assumptions regarding statistical tests, such as normality of distribution, are violated, when measures used are unreliable, and the range on a variable is narrow. Additionally, when investigators go on a fishing expedition and run multiple comparisons in pursuit of finding associations or differences, these multiple tests of hypotheses increases the probability that one of the tests will be significant.[1] One way to maintain the family-wise error rate or the chance of rejecting the null hypothesis when it is true (Type I error), is to perform a Bonferonni correction, named for Italian mathematician Carlo Emilio Bonferroni, or Šidàk approach.[1] The null hypothesis is rejected if we observe a *rare* event, but the more tests performed, say 5 or more, the more likely it is to find rare events and mistakenly believe that there is an effect when there is none.[1] For example, if you wanted to examine differences between genders on all polysomnographic parameters, you would increase the likelihood of finding differences just by virtue of the number of t-tests performed. This is called *inflation* of the alpha level. Making the alpha level more stringent (i.e., smaller) using the Bonferroni- Šidàk approach will create less errors, but make it harder to detect real effects.[1] Another threat to statistical validity is when the implementation of the intervention is unreliable. This can be assessed with inter- and intra-rater reliability. The planned statistical analysis assumes that the variance generated by the intervention is stable. If the implementation of the intervention varies, so will the variance and this will be a source of error. Moreover, there may be extraneous variance in the experimental setting that needs to be considered. For example, if you are examining the relationship between performance on a sustained attention task and sleep deprivation, an interruption while the task is being performed, such as a fire alarm, would affect the participant's ability to sustain attention, an additional source of variance that would not be present otherwise and extraneous to the effect of daytime sleepiness on performance. Of course an inaccurate estimation of the effect size, which determines the sample size, will also pose a threat to statistical conclusion validity.

Internal validity reflects the validity of the inferences about whether the observed covariation between A (presumed treatment) and B (presumed outcome) reflects a causal relationship between A and B as these variables are manipulated or measured. As internal validity is only applicable where there are assumptions regarding causal relationships, it usually is not applicable in observational or descriptive studies.[2] Ambiguous temporal precedence, or the inability to determine which variable was the cause and which was the effect, is a contributing factor to undermining internal validity. The biases that may result in the selection of comparison groups can also pose a threat to internal validity, such as comparing groups that have different ages, genders, or level of disease severity. A second threat to internal validity is history. This includes specific events that occur between the first and second measurement that might affect the cause effect relationship between the independent and dependent variable. The longer the duration of time, the more likely events that occur between measurements may have an effect on the outcome measure. Similar to the threat of history, maturation is the threat that occurs when within subject processes, such as a change in health status, with the passage of time. The longer the time between data collection at baseline and post-intervention, the greater is this treat to the validity of the results. Moreover, with the passage of time, there is the possibility, depending on the outcome measure, that participants may improve their performance on the metric, regardless of treatment.

Another consideration is the effect of regression to the mean on the validity of the findings. This threat occurs when participants are selected on the basis of extreme scores or characteristics. To illustrate this consideration, following is an example from the sleep research field. Participants with severe obstructive sleep apnea (OSA) are more likely to show improvement after one night of continuous positive airway pressure (CPAP) than those with more moderate disease. This threat also applies when values obtained for screening participants for the study are also used as the baseline values. To avoid this threat, separate assessments should be performed to obtain screening and baseline data for the same variable. That is, scores at baseline should not also be used to determine enrollment into the study. As the chance of obtaining a significant finding is also based on the number of participants relative to the statistical test used, loss of participants will increase the risk of not finding statistical significance. The loss of participants in a study is known as attrition and a proportion of participants should be added to the total sample size to account for the loss. A rule of thumb is if the study is 3 months or less, plan for a 10 percent drop in participation; a 15 percent drop would be expected in studies of greater than 3 months. Of course this depends on the nature of participant burden as greater burden will likely result in higher attrition levels. The threat of testing denotes the effect of taking a test once on the outcomes of taking the test a second time. Therefore, baseline testing does have an impact on performance on the final outcome assessment, depending on the length of time between tests. This threat can be mitigated, by including the baseline score in the analysis of differences when examining change between pre- and post-intervention. This is also a good approach when there may be differences in baseline scores between the two comparison groups.

Changes in the instrument, observers, or scorers may produce changes in outcomes and poses an internal threat in addition to posing a threat to statistical conclusion validity. Assessing the reliability and stability of a measure and inter- and intra-rater reliability of observers and scorers, especially related to polysomnography, is essential to obtaining quality data and accurate findings. There may also be additive and interactive effects of measurement as well as other aspects of the protocol that needs to be considered. Finally, the John Henry effect is also a threat to internal validity. John Henry was a worker who outperformed a machine in an experiment because he was aware that his performance was compared to that of the machine.[3] It is the effect that occurs when participants in the control group view itself as being in a competition with the treatment group and this changes their behavior. This is the difference between the John Henry effect and the more common Hawthorne effect where the knowledge of being in a study affects behavior and thus has an impact on the results of that study.[3] The Hawthorne effect comes from the Hawthorne Works, a factory complex in Cicero, Illinois, where a series of studies were carried out on factory workers between 1924 and 1932.[3] Researchers increased light intensity in the factory and found that worker productivity increased, but they also found that productivity increased when they reduced light intensity.

If the conceptual framework or conceptual definitions of key variables are not well articulated then the design can suffer from threats to construct validity. **Construct validity** is the degree to which inferences can legitimately be made because the operationalizations of the study stem from the theoretical constructs on which those operationalizations were based.[4] This allows for generalization of your findings conceptually to other studies using similar concepts.[4] This may be perceived as a "labeling" issue.[4] For example, if you are measuring "sleepiness", is this manifest sleepiness, physiologic sleepiness, or fatigue? Well-designed studies are conceptually conceived. Problems with construct validity occur when there is inadequate explication of the constructs. These flaws are less likely when salient variables are derived and defined by the conceptual underpinnings of the research or if multiple levels of a concept are tested and not just one level, e.g., different doses of a medication.[5] Mono-operation bias, another threat, occurs when conceptually irrelevant constructs are operationally defined. On the other hand, mono-method bias is the term applied when the conceptual and operational definitions are the same, e.g., self-report, or if only one method is used to measure the concept.[5] Using only one measure will draw the criticism that you are only measuring one aspect of the concept.[5] Multiple methods of measuring the key concepts and using pilot data to indicate that the measures behave in a conceptually-consistent fashion will help to mitigate this threat.[5] There are two issues with regard to testing that will affect construct validity. The first occurs when the properties of the measure change as a result of the intervention. The alteration in psychometric or structural properties may be hidden and thus difficult to detect. The second is when the metric itself makes the groups more sensitive or receptive to the intervention.[5] Treatment diffusion is present when there is an undetectable intervention aside from the intended intervention that may have an effect on the dependent variable. When unanticipated consequences, such as side effects, occur in a positive intervention study, it may be inaccurate to consider the intervention effective and may restrict the generalizability of the treatment.[5] Similar to the John Henry and Hawthorne effects, participants may try to guess the hypothesis and concentrate on certain performance areas with increased motivation if they believe those are the focus of the study. Likewise, participants may also be concerned about being evaluated and this "testing anxiety" might also influence the outcome of the study.[5] Other participant perspectives that might alter the study include compensatory rivalry ("bring it on"!) and resentful demoralization ("but I wanted X treatment"). Sometimes, the comparison group is treated differently receiving some form of compensation to make up for the fact that they are not receiving the intervention. This is called compensatory equalization. Finally, the investigator in their desire for significant results may consciously or unconsciously affect the results of the study.[5] It is for these experimenter expectancies that the principal investigator and those delivering the intervention should be blinded, if possible, not involved in data collection, and have limited or no interaction with participants.[5]

External validity is the threat that influences the generalizability of the study, which is the extent to which the results of your study would hold for other persons, other places and other times.[6] For example, there may be a causal interaction between characteristics of the sample that produced results that would not be replicable in another sample. This is especially problematic when the sample is not randomly selected. There can also be an interaction of causal relationship and treatment variation such that one variation of the treatment may not hold for other variations or when combined with other treatments. This may also be the case with outcome observations and measures, known as the interaction of causal relationship with treatment outcomes. The effect produced by one type of outcome observation or measure may not hold if other outcome observations or metrics are used. There would also be limits to generalizability with changes in settings from the original research, known as interactions of causal relationship with setting. What works for one setting, such as a sleep laboratory, may not produce the same results obtained in another setting, such as the home. In the situation of context-dependent mediation, variables that are explanatory mediators of a relationship in one context, may not mediate in another. As we will discuss below, controlling these factors is key to enhancing the quality of the study and the extent to which it can apply to other persons, places, and times.

TYPES OF HUMAN STUDIES

SURVEY RESEARCH

The primary techniques used in survey research are survey techniques and interviews. Surveys can be administered by mail, telephone, in a group setting, or household drop-off where the investigator goes to the home and leaves the survey in the hands of the respondent.[7] Another example is exhibited in **Table 1**. The difference between a survey and a questionnaire is that a survey does not undergo the rigorous psychometric testing for validity and reliability that is conducted on a questionnaire. Interviews may be conducted in person, via telephone, or include focus groups.[7] Both the survey and interview may be composed of closed or open ended questions or a mix of these types.[7] Selecting the appropriate method, survey versus interview, will depend on how well the population can be defined and accessed, presence of language issues, potential problems with response rates, types and sequence of the questions asked, content issues, potential biases such as socially desirable responses, control of interviewer distortion or subversion, the problem of false respondents, and such administrative issues as cost, facilities, time, and personnel.[8]

QUASI-EXPERIMENTAL DESIGNS (see **Table 1**)

Three aspects of research design differentiate the gold standard experimental from quasi-experimental study – randomization, control, and manipulation (i.e., intervention or treatment). These factors, described more fully below, mitigate the threats to validity avoiding Type I and II errors and enabling wider generalization of the findings. Additionally, the true experiment uses two concurrent groups and controls for crucial variables that may affect the interpretation of the findings regarding causal relationships. There are several limitations or obstacles that influence the investigator's decision to use a quasi-experimental design. There may be ethical issues that prevent randomization or manipulation. For example, many early studies examining the effect of CPAP treatment in OSA were quasi-experimental designs because it was believed that denying participants of treatment was putting them at risk for

Table 1 Examples of Survey, Quasi-Experimental, and Experimental Designs

Type of Design	Example
Survey Research	
Survey	Bixler, E. O., A. N. Vgontzas, et al. (1998). Effects of age on sleep apnea in men: I. Prevalence and severity. Am J Respir Crit Care Med 157(1): 144-8.
Quasi-Experimental Design	
One Group Pre-Test, Post-Test	Weaver, T. E., G. Maislin, et al. (2007). Relationship between hours of CPAP use and achieving normal levels of sleepiness and daily functioning. *SLEEP* 30(6): 711-9.
Reversed Time series	Kribbs, N. B., A. I. Pack, et al. (1993). Effects of one night without nasal CPAP treatment on sleep and sleepiness in patients with obstructive sleep apnea. Am Rev Respir Dis 147(5): 1162-8.
Retrospective design	Moul DE, Nofzinger EA, Pilkonis PA, Houck PR, Miewald JM, Buysse DJ. Symptom reports in severe chronic insomnia. *SLEEP*. 2002;25(5):553-63.
Experimental Design	
Pre-test, Post-test, Parallel Groups	Fava, M., et al., Zolpidem extended-release improves sleep and next-day symptoms in comorbid insomnia and generalized anxiety disorder. J Clin Psychopharmacol, 2009. 29(3): p. 222-30.
Cross-Over Design	Taibi, D.M., et al., A randomized clinical trial of valerian fails to improve self-reported, polysomnographic, and actigraphic sleep in older women with insomnia. Sleep Med, 2009. 10(3): p. 319-28.

sleepiness-related adverse events. Pre-existing groups may also prevent randomization to experiment and control groups. There may also be conditions that make it impossible to prevent contamination of the intervention group in an experimental design. The experimental design also may require more participants than are available. A quasi-experimental design often requires fewer subjects. Finally, the independent variable may not be able to be controlled or manipulated to enable the exploration of a casual relationship.

The simplest quasi-experimental designs are the **post-test only or the one group pre-test, post-test design**. These designs are depicted below with X indicating the intervention and O the observation. In the **post-test only** design, there is no baseline assessment with only an outcome evaluation after the intervention. In the one-group pre-test, post-test design, baseline data collection occurs prior to the intervention followed by the outcome assessment. The pre-test strengthens this design as it allows the determination of differences between groups pre-interventions. Those variables on which the two groups differ can then be controlled statistically.

Post-Test Only:

X O

One Group Pre-Test, Post-Test:

$$O_1 \; X \; O_2$$

Terry Weaver, PhD and Connie M. Ulrich, PhD

Threats to validity associated with the pre-post-test design include history, maturation and testing. The effect of giving the pre-test itself may also affect the outcomes of the second evaluation and statistical conclusion validity. When there are different levels of the dependent variable and/or other important variables at the start of the study, then the design of **non-equivalent groups, post-test** or **pre-test, post-test non-equivalent groups** only are applied. This design is shown below.

Post-Test Only, Non-Equivalent Groups:

$$X \ O$$
$$\overline{}$$
$$O$$

Pre-test, Post-test, Non-Equivalent Groups:

$$O_1 \ X \ O_2$$
$$\overline{}$$
$$O_1 \quad O_2$$

As the groups are not randomly assigned, this design suffers from the threat of selection in addition to mortality. If the investigator wants to explore changes with treatment over time or when only one group is available, a time series design, displayed below, might be employed. Compared to a parallel groups design, a smaller sample size can often be used with the time series design; there is repeated measurement, and all participants receive the intervention. The reverse time series design is commonly used to assess the efficacy of an intervention. In this design, the intervention is introduced, effects measured, and then the treatment is withdrawn (W) to ascertain whether symptoms return. With both of these designs, there is concern regarding testing and intra- and inter-rater reliability; every effort should be made to standardize measurements. However, as measurements are taken intermittently, it does provide control over natural processes of maturation or the disease process. This design is not optimal in situations where the course is unstable such as with natural remissions or exacerbations.

Time Series:
$$O_1 \ O_2 \ O_3 \ O_4 \ X \ O_5 \ O_6 \ O_7 \ O_8$$
Reversed Time Series:
$$O_1 \ O_2 \ X \ O_3 \ O_4 \ WX \ O_5 \ O_6 \ X \ O_7 \ O_8$$

The **cross-over design** is an approach used in both quasi-experimental and experimental designs. In the quasi-experimental design, this is a type of time series design. All participants get all treatments, but the two groups get the treatments in a different order.

Crossover:
$$S_1: O_1 \ X_1 \ O_2........O_3 \ X_2 \ O_4$$
$$S_2: O_1 \ X_2 \ O_2........O_3 \ X_1 \ O_4$$

The assessment of the interventions would be conducted by comparing the mean of time one with the mean of time two for each treatment, i.e., X_1 at Time 1 with X_2 at Time 2. If differences are detected, this would indicate an order effect or the indication that the order in which the treatments were presented made a difference and affected the results. Although an order effect is not always desirable, it may be important information for future studies. In trying to determine factors that might be related to an important variable or intervention, the **non-concurrent control group** design allows the investigator to examine putative variables prospectively, i.e., forward from the point of assessment, or retrospectively, back after the point of assessment. As the initial assessment is made on a different group, at a different time from the one evaluated prospectively or retrospectively, the predominant threat to this design is history. There is the potential that different historic events could affect each group.

Prospective – start here and move forward:

x ⟶

Retrospective – go back and see what factors correlate:

◄——— x ———►

In summary, the quasi-experimental design is more practical, feasible, and generalizable than the experimental design because it often requires fewer subjects and requires fewer restrictions, thus permitting greater generalizability. However, as there is less control, the quasi-experimental design has a greater chance of bias, less internal validity, and more alternative explanations for results than the hypothesized causal relationship.

EXPERIMENTAL DESIGNS (see **Table 1**)

As discussed above, the experimental design (Level 1) is considered the most robust design in science and one that generates the highest level of evidence that demonstrates the effect of one variable on another. It also provides the greatest control over the threats to internal validity. However, disadvantages are artificial conditions may be imposed limiting the external validity and ability to widely generalize the findings. There is also the greater risk of introducing Hawthorne or John Henry effects. One outcome variable is usually the target of interest, limiting the number of variables that can be evaluated. Given the participant burden associated with this design, there may also be greater attrition. Experimental designs are prospective and compare the effect of an intervention(s) against a control. Used in studies to evaluate prophylactic, diagnostic, and therapeutic agents, regimens, procedures and devices, this design involves random assignment to either the treatment or control group. There must be at least two concurrent groups with at least one comparison – one dependent treatment variable and one independent outcome variable. Another requirement is that of manipulation; one group gets the intervention (experimental group) and the other does not (control or placebo group). The performance of the control group on the dependent variable is the basis for evaluating performance of the experimental group. The primary or important variables or endpoint is identified and determines whether the intervention was a success or failure with participants followed from a well-defined point. Other outcome variables are considered secondary endpoints.

PHASES OF CLINICAL TRIALS

In the development of an intervention, several steps or phases must occur before it is ready for widespread implementation.[9] There are four phases. Phase 1 is used when developing the drug, biologic, or device and is designed to increase the understanding of how well the intervention can be tolerated, that is the maximum dose that can be tolerated before unacceptable toxicity occurs (maximally tolerated dose[MTD]).[9] The MTD is determined by starting with a very low dose and increasing the dose until a predetermined level of intolerance occurs.[9] Using a step-up approach, usually a small number of participants are enrolled, typically 3, are entered sequentially at a particular dose. If unacceptable toxicity is observed, additional patients are enrolled at the same dose and escalation of the dose continues if not further toxicity is observed. If

 Terry Weaver, PhD and Connie M. Ulrich, PhD

unacceptable toxicity occurs, then escalation is halted and that or the previous dose is declared the MTD.[9] This design is based on the presumption that the MTD occurs when approximately one third of participants experience an unacceptable toxicity.[9] The next step is the Phase II study. The goal of this phase is to evaluate whether the pharmaceutical has biologic activity or effect and to estimate the rate of adverse events in order to determine the right dose for maximal effectiveness with minimal side effects. In this design a minimal level of activity, for example 20 percent, may be the threshold for moving forward with further testing.[9] It is the Phase III study that determines efficacy of the intervention in a more general population and thus its role in clinical practice.[9] This phase is often multisite involving large number of participants followed for a short period of time.[9] The Phase IV trial determines long-term safety. Considered the "open label" phase of agent or device development, this design tests the intervention in a new population and over a longer period of time.

When designing the experiment, there are several focal considerations. First, the study population should be determined and well defined with specific inclusion and exclusion criteria identified. Enrollment procedures, including generation of the consent document and obtaining informed consent, along with assessment of eligibility and intervention allocation should be spelled out in as much detail as possible. Finally, follow-up visits need to be specifically described and the schedule determined. All of these pieces should reflect the primary aim and be designed to test the hypothesis(es). These aspects of the design are articulated in the study protocol that is then used to produce the procedure manual.

TYPES OF RANDOMIZATION

When properly executed, random assignment should produce comparable study groups with respect to known and unknown characteristics, removes investigator bias, and guarantees that significance tests will have valid significance levels.[9] The most common randomization strategy is fixed randomization. Here, participants have a pre-specified probability, usually an equal chance, and that probability is not altered during the study.[9] There are several approaches to fixed allocation – simple, blocked, and stratified. The simplest form of fixed randomization is the coin toss where the coin is tossed to determine treatment allocation whenever a participant is eligible to be randomized.[9] Another common practice is the random digit table where the equally likely digits 0 to 9 are arranged by rows and columns.[9] Random selection of a certain column of numbers and using the sequence of digits such as Group A would be assigned to those participants for whom the next digit in the column was even and Group B to those for whom the next digit was odd.[9] This process results in a sequence of assignments that is random in order with each participant having an equal chance of being assigned to either Group A or Group B.[9] The determination of which group is treatment and which is the control can be done with a flip of the coin. For small studies, the sealed opaque envelope technique can be used. Beginning with the same number of opaque envelopes as the required sample size, the envelopes are divided with half containing a card indicating Group A and the other half containing a card or Group B. The cards are shuffled and put into a container (for example a hat) and an envelope is drawn when each participant is eligible for randomization. It is essential to use an opaque envelope for the integrity of this approach to be maintained. It may be tempting for an investigator to hold the envelope up to the light to see the allocation of the participant and alter the allocation sequence. However, most studies, especially large studies, use the more convenient computer executed random number-producing algorithm to determine the randomization schedule.[9]

To guarantee an even distribution of participants between the experimental and treatment group, you would use blocked randomization by "blocking" on the desired variable. Blocked randomization prevents an imbalance in the number of participants assigned to the experimental versus control group by specifying an allocation ratio (such as 1:1 or 2:1) after every "block" of specified size.[10] For example, a block of a specified size, such as12, would contain 6 A and 6 B with a ratio of 1:1 or 8 A and 4 B with a ratio of 2:1.[10] The generation of the randomization sequence involves randomly selecting from all the permutations of assignments that meet the specified ratio.[10] If you want the experimental and control groups to equally represent a specific characteristic, perhaps one that would confound the results like age, then stratified randomization would be used to achieve comparability between study groups.[9] These factors should be measured either before or at the time of randomization[9] and strata or subgroups are generated for each stratified variable. If stratification is desired for several factors, a stratum is formed by selecting one subgroup for each factor.[9] In this case, the total number of strata is the product of the number of subgroups in each factor. Using the example of age, the strata could be 30 – 39, 40 – 50, 51 – 60 years. If gender is added as a stratum then the design has 3 X 2 = 6 strata. Randomization is conducted within strata. However, most clinical trials use blocked randomization to assure an even distribution of the participants among the two treatment groups and strata.[9]

DESIGNS (see Table 1)

The post-test only, pre-test/post-test, and cross-over (single or double) experimental designs are the same as depicted above in the discussion of quasi-experimental designs except that there is randomization of the participants to the two groups with one group serving as the experimental and the other the control group. If the cross-over design is used, there is the concern that the effect of one intervention will not be completely eliminated, or "washed out" affecting the response to the second intervention. It is critical, then, to be sure that there is sufficient time to wash out the effect of the first intervention before crossing over and introducing the second.

A derivation of the pre-test/post-test design is the **Solomon Four Design**. As discussed above, testing in of itself may affect the outcome independent of the intervention. The aim of this design is to specifically determine the effect of baseline testing on the post-intervention results. As illustrated below, participants are randomly assigned to one of four groups, two experimental and two control. Only one of the experimental and control groups receives pre-testing so that differences in response to the treatment can be evaluated in terms of whether the group received pre-testing or not. This then allows the investigator to control for the variance attributed to testing in the final determination of the variance between the experimental and control group related to the intervention.

Experimental 1	R	O_1 X	O_2
Experimental 2	R	X	O_2
Control 1	R	O_1	O_2
Control 2	R		O_2

The **factorial design** is used when each factor has two or more levels such as gender (male/female). This design permits testing of multiple hypotheses as well as evaluate main effects and interactions. For example, perhaps you would like to evaluate the effect of a pharmaceutical agent on daytime sleepiness, but want to see if there are gender differences with regard to response to treatment. The factorial design, as shown below, would have two treatment groups (control and experimental) and two levels of gender. With the factorial design, there is random assignment within cells as would be the case with stratified randomization.

Terry Weaver, PhD and Connie M. Ulrich, PhD

Group	Intervention	
	Individual	Class
Experimental Men		X
Control Men	X	
Experimental Women		X
Control Women	X	

In this example, you would compare the experimental groups with the control groups. You could also compare the experimental men with the control men, and the experimental women with the control women.

BASELINE ASSESSMENT

As the aim of clinical trials is the intervention-control comparison, the same data is collected at two points in time – at baseline and post-intervention. This comparison should not be made using data not collected prior to the intervention.[9] The amount of data collected at baseline should be kept to a minimum as analyses using the primary endpoint are the only ones that address the primary hypothesis and thus essential.[9] Additional data collected at baseline should be limited to pertinent demographic and medical variables.[9] Collecting large amounts of baseline data also adds to participant burden.[9] A balance should be struck, then, between participant burden and the conduct of secondary analyses.

ETHICAL CONCERNS

Ethical issues arise in the conduct of research because human subjects voluntarily participate in experimental and/or other types of interventional research studies as a means to advance scientific knowledge of specific disease entities that impact the morbidity and mortality of human illness. The U.S. Federal Guidelines (45CFR46.102), or Common Rule, defines a *human subject* as:

"A living individual about whom an investigator (whether professional or student) conducting research obtains (1) data through intervention or interaction with the individual, or (2) identifiable private information.[11]

Randomized controlled trials (RCT) are conducted to determine the safety, efficacy, and effectiveness of two or more health-related or pharmacological interventions. Every participant in an RCT is randomly assigned and thus has an equal opportunity to be in any arm of the study under investigation. *Intervention* includes "both physical procedures by which data are gathered (for example, venipuncture) and manipulations of the subject or the subject's environment that are performed for research purposes. Interaction includes communication or interpersonal contact between investigator and subject. *Private information* includes information about behavior that occurs in a context in which an individual can reasonably expect that no observation or recording is taking place, and information which has been provided for specific purposes by an individual and which the individual can reasonably expect will not be made public (for example, a medical record). Private information must be individually identifiable (i.e., the identity of the subject is or may readily be ascertained by the investigator or associated with the information) in order for obtaining the information to constitute research involving human subjects."[11,12]

In their landmark article on *"What makes clinical research ethical?"* Emanuel, Wendler and Grady[13] outline a comprehensive and systematic research ethics framework for researchers, bioethicists, institutional review boards, and others to use when evaluating the ethical integrity of clinical research (**Table 2**).

Table 2 Guidelines for Ethical Clinical Research

Social or scientific value
- What is the research question and how will it advance sleep medicine?
- Is the research question novel, generalizable, and translatable to clinical practice?

Scientific validity
- What is the most appropriate study design and statistical measure(s) to address the research question(s)?
- Is there a true null hypothesis where controversy exists in the professional sleep community and/or individual investigator as to whether the intervention is better than the standard therapy, including placebo?

Fair subject selection
- Are the inclusion and exclusion criteria clearly defined and justifications provided as needed (e.g., enrollment of vulnerable or marginalized subjects?)

Favorable risk-benefit ratio
- Are the potential benefits and burdens (e.g., physical, psychological, economic, social) delineated clearly for individual participants?
- Are the potential benefits enhanced and burdens/risks minimized?
- If benefits are minimal, does the knowledge yield to be derived from the study justify the risks?

Independent review
- Has the research protocol been vetted through the appropriate institutional review board and has the process been transparent?
- Is there a need for multiple independent reviews?
- Is a study monitor and/or Data Safety and Monitoring Board required?

Informed consent
- Is there full disclosure of the elements of informed consent? (i.e., purpose, risks/benefits, alternatives, compensation, voluntariness, methods/procedures, right to withdraw consent without penalty).
- Is the informed consent process sensitive to the participant's culture, language, and context?
- Is there a need for proxy or community consent?

Respect for potential and enrolled participant
- Are individual participants aware that they can withdraw from the study at any given point without penalty?
- Are issues of confidentiality and privacy adequately addressed?
- Will results of the research be shared with participants; what if new information becomes available during the course of the research, will that be shared with subjects?
- How will the overall study findings be disseminated?

(Emanuel, E., Wendler, D., and Grady, C. "What Makes Clinical Research Ethical?" *JAMA*, 283, 20 (May 24, 2000): 2701-2711).

Ethical issues inherent in clinical research designs associated with sleep medicine or other types of clinical specialties can include ethical controversies surrounding equipoise, placebo and sham procedures, blinding, and treatment failures.

WHAT IS EQUIPOISE AND WHY IS IT ETHICALLY CONTROVERSIAL?

For a randomized controlled trial to be ethically justifiable, there must be an honest null hypothesis (i.e., scientifically valid research question to be studied) and what is referred to as a state of equipoise.[14-18] Equipoise is "an ethical condition of all controlled clinical trials, whether or not they are randomized, placebo-controlled, or blinded."[14] This means that it is not known if the experimental intervention in arm A is superior when compared to an established intervention (i.e., standard of care) in arm B or to no treatment at all (untreated control group). Equipoise was first discussed by Charles Fried[19] and Benjamin Freedman[14] more than twenty years ago. Several authors have defined equipoise in the research context, including theoretical or individual equipoise as well as collective or clinical equipoise.

Fried's conception of *individual* or *theoretical* equipoise basically relied on the ethical integrity and professional judgment of individual investigators (e.g., physicians) to determine either from the literature, their own thoughts, feelings, and gut instincts, or other sources whether a state of equipoise existed for them to recommend enrollment of research subjects in a randomized clinical trial.[14-19] Because of the unique fiduciary relationship that exists between a patient and his or her physician, Fried argued that investigators should not enroll subjects in a randomized clinical trial if they believe there is a specific preference for one treatment option over the other. As many investigators are also physicians, this blending of roles can violate their ethical obligation to act in the best interest of the patient and to recommend the best known therapy at the time of the patient-physician encounter. For an investigator to be in equipoise Markman[20] claimed that he or she should be willing to enroll him or herself or a family member in the trial; however, personal experience, interpretation of data, or even specific knowledge of the patient's condition can lead the investigator to prefer one treatment over the other.[21] Thus, it is easy to see how tenuous individual equipoise is and how it can create moral tension as both patients and physicians can change their views based on the benefits and burdens experienced in a single clinical trial.[21]

To resolve the inherent tension between research and personal care, Freedman argued for a different conception of equipoise—*clinical equipoise*.[14] Instead of relying solely on an individual physician to determine the relative merits of a clinical trial and whether patient participation is ethically acceptable, Freedman argued for a broader professional dialogue and consensus from a community of scholars within the particular field of study. According to Freedman, clinical equipoise exists when there is, "genuine uncertainty within the expert medical community—not necessarily on the part of the individual investigator—about the preferred treatment."[14] Since Freedom proposed clinical equipoise in 1987, the majority of the research community advocates this ethical and scientific principle as the most widely accepted norm of RCTs; yet it is not without its critics.

Some authors have suggested alternative approaches to equipoise as well as simply abandoning the principle all together. For example, Miller and Brody[16,17] recommend the use of a non-exploitation framework to protect human subjects (i.e., respecting the rights of patient-subjects and judging the relative merits of the proposed trial by the ethical criteria outlined by Emanuel and colleagues) because they believe that clinical equipoise confuses the "ethics of clinical research" with the "ethics of clinical medicine" and the two are uniquely distinct activities as described in the Belmont Report (**Table 3**).[22] Needless to say, equipoise remains a controversial issue, but the ultimate goal is to design methodologically rigorous clinical trials that address scientifically valid research questions that aim to protect the rights of human subjects who participate for the benefit of others.

PLACEBOS, SHAM INTERVENTIONS, AND BLINDING PROCEDURES IN SLEEP MEDICINE

Similar to the ethical concerns surrounding equipoise, the use of placebos and sham interventions in randomized clinical trials also raise significant ethical issues in the conduct of research. When designing a clinical sleep study, the investigator may choose to "have no control group, a placebo or sham control group, a usual-care group, an active treatment group using an approved therapy or intervention, or a control group that receives "best available therapy."[23]

A placebo is a chemically inert substance that is given deliberately to subjects participating in randomized placebo-controlled trials as a means to rigorously test treatment efficacy; the placebo's pharmacological

Table 3 1978: Belmont Report Definitions of Research and Practice for the Protection of Human Subjects

Concept	Definition
Research	"An activity designed to test a hypothesis, permit conclusions to be drawn, and thereby to develop or contribute to generalizable knowledge (expressed, for example, in theories, principles, and statements of relationships). Research is usually described in a formal protocol that sets forth an objective and a set of procedures designed to reach that objective."
Practice	"Interventions that are designed solely to enhance the well-being of an individual patient or client and that have a reasonable expectation of success. The purpose of medical or behavioral practice is to provide diagnosis, preventive treatment, or therapy to particular individuals."

activity is not specifically designated as a treatment for the disease under study although it may have known or unknown effects on the patient-subject's disease or symptoms (known as the placebo effect).[24, 25] Castro identifies several important reasons for designing clinical studies including a placebo control group. This is because: (a) It is the most methodologically rigorous means to test treatment efficacy; (b) fewer patient-subjects can be enrolled which minimizes their potential exposure to ineffective or toxic treatments; (c) the value of "adding on" the placebo group to standard of care in comparison to the experimental intervention added to standard of care more adequately evaluates the risk or benefit of the experimental intervention; and (d) it controls bias from subjective outcome measures (e.g., depression, symptoms). Additionally, blinding or treatment masking procedures help to control investigator, research staff, and patient bias regarding treatment assignment and experimental outcomes.[26] In a single-blinded study, patient-subjects are unaware of their treatment assignment; and in a double-blinded study, both the investigator and patient-subject are unaware if the patient-subject is receiving the experimental substance under investigation or the placebo.[26]

The Declaration of Helsinki[27] is an international document developed by the World Medical Assembly (WMA) in 1964 and provides physician investigators and others in the research community with a collective set of guidelines for the ethical conduct of research with human subjects.[27] The document has been revised several times with the most controversial statement stemming from Article 29 in October 2000 surrounding the use of placebos in clinical trials:

"The benefits, risks, burden and effectiveness of a new method should be tested against those of the best current prophylactic, diagnostic and therapeutic methods. This does not exclude the use of placebo, or not treatment, in studies where no proven prophylactic, diagnostic or therapeutic method exists."

The seemingly apparent prohibition of placebo-controlled trials when the best proven effective therapy exists created much controversy for the research and bioethics community. As such, a Note of Clarification was made to Article 29 in 2002 and states the following, "The WMA hereby reaffirms its position that extreme care must be taken in making use of a placebo-controlled trial and that in general this methodology should only be used in the absence of existing proven therapy. However, a placebo-controlled trial may be ethically acceptable, even if proven therapy is available, under the following circumstances: (a) Where for compelling and scientifically sound methodological reasons its use is necessary to determine the efficacy or safety of a prophylactic, diagnostic or therapeutic method; or (b) Where a prophylactic, diagnostic or therapeutic method is being investigated for a minor condition and the patients who receive placebo will not be subject to any additional risk of serious or irreversible."[27]

A sham arm is one type of control option in RCTs designed to test the efficacy of a particular device or procedural treatment. Sham procedures can be very controversial depending on the risk level and degree of invasiveness (e.g., sham surgery) as subjects in the sham control arm are meant to experience the same accompanying effects as those who are actually going through the true procedure.[28-31] As such, Sutherland[29] argues that subjects enrolled in a sham arm may experience discomfort or risk not typically experienced by those who receive an inert substance in a standard placebo-controlled drug trial. Clinician-investigators may also experience moral discomfort as they are not usually blinded in a sham control trial because they must manipulate the study procedures to maintain the subject's sense of "realness" associated with the protocol. Horng and Miller[31] suggest that sham procedures can be ethically justified but they must meet certain criteria. These considerations include: (a) The importance of the research question to be studied and the risks to subjects of the placebo and/or sham control are justified by the knowledge to be gained; (b) the placebo or sham control arm is necessary to test the study hypothesis; (c) risks to subjects in the sham control or placebo group are minimized to the extent possible and/or reasonable with respect to the benefits, if any to be gained; and (d) the informed consent document outlines specific procedures related to the sham/placebo group and subjects understand and voluntarily accept the possibility of placebo or sham assignment through their participation.

TREATMENT FAILURES, UNDERPOWERED STUDIES, AND EXTERNAL MONITORING

The outcome of a clinical trial can either be treatment success or treatment failure. Treatment failures pose significant ethical concerns because human subjects are exposed to the risks and toxicities of experimental treatments without the potential for future benefit, limiting valid conclusions. Treatment failures can occur in randomized controlled trials for various reasons. First, many studies are simply underpowered to determine treatment effects; hence, the researcher wrongly concludes that the null hypothesis is true (no significant difference exists between the study arms) when in fact it is false. For example, this can be the case when there are too small numbers of research participants in the experimental arm to detect clinically meaningful effects.

"The power of a study is its probability of detecting a clinically important effect of the experimental treatment, compared with the control arm, if a difference actually exists."[32] Generally, a power analysis is conducted for two purposes: (a) To determine the appropriate sample size needed to demonstrate significance, which avoids wasting finite resources; and (b) to determine the power of a statistical test post hoc.[33] Additionally, each human subject who voluntarily chooses to enroll in a research study has the right to know how many subjects will actually be participating in the study, among other factors; and, an a priori power analysis provides justification for the sample size outlined in the informed consent document. In doing so, the ethical principle of respect for persons is upheld because individuals have the autonomous right to determine what is in their best interest after all information related to the research has been disclosed and they have carefully weighed the benefits and burdens of research participation.

Halpern, Karlawish, and Berlin[34] as well as other authors suggest that even when the researcher has conducted an appropriate a priori power analysis a failure to recruit or retain the stated number of research subjects can affect the overall scientific validity of the study, ultimately, limiting the generalizability of the data. External monitoring is often required to assess certain aspects of a study, including recruitment and retention and especially trials that involve interventions and are deemed greater than minimal risk. The type of monitoring that is required depends on the following:

- Phase of clinical trial
- Risk level
- Blinding procedures
- Multisite or single site study

For example, a multi-centered, large Phase III clinical trial that is assessing the effectiveness of a new insomnia medication (that might cause adverse effects) for those individuals who have difficulty sleeping would require the appointment of a Data and Safety Monitoring Board (DSMB). The DSMB consists of several individual members who are completely independent of the study investigator and sponsor and include scientific experts in the field of study and trial design, ethicists, and biostatisticians, among others.[35] There are two major responsibilities of a DSMB: (1): to protect the safety of human subjects; and (2) to ensure the overall integrity of the study (http://grants.nih.gov/grants/guide/notice-files/r.ot98-084.html). Specifically, a DSMB will make recommendations about:

- Risk/benefit ratio
- Participant safety and participant burden
- Efficacy of the study intervention
- Recruitment and retention of human subjects
- Quality of study, including adherence to study procedures and performance of center sites
- Amendments to study protocol

A DSMB can suggest that the study continue as planned, propose modifications to improve the informed consent documents and enhance subject recruitment or safety, or advise early stopping of the trial (i.e., if the intervention is clearly beneficial, the risks outweigh the benefits, or if subjects are exposed to risk without a reasonable chance of detecting significant differences).

SUMMARY

The ultimate goal of research is to improve the human condition through scientific advancement and understanding of various disease entities. Ultimately investigators are responsible for the ethical conduct of their research. Thinking through the ethical challenges of designing clinical research studies—blinding, sham or placebo controls, and equipoise—will assist investigators in producing methodologically rigorous outcomes that respect human subjects in the process of their contribution to research.

STATISTICAL CONCERNS

SAMPLE SIZE DETERMINATION

There are two important points when considering sample size. First, as described above, the sample size should be sufficient to provide enough statistical power to demonstrate differences between the two groups.[9] The other important point is that the number of participants in the sample size are the number who finish the trial not the number who enter the trial.[36] The sample size determination will be based on the statistic that will be used in the data analysis to test the hypothesis. The first step in determining the sample size is the identification of the primary endpoint or response variable. These typically fall into three types: dichotomous response variables, such as success or failure, where the event rates are compared between the intervention and the control group; continuous response variables, such as blood pressure or questionnaire scores, where the

Terry Weaver, PhD and Connie M. Ulrich, PhD

mean level or change of the intervention group is compared with the mean level or change of the control group; time to failure or the occurrence of a clinical event where a hazard rate is used.[9] Most often, the information that is needed in the determination of the sample size includes: (a) The magnitude of the effect expected or desired, (b) variability of the variables being analyzed, and (c) the desired probability (power) of observing that effect with a defined significance level.[36] The power selected is often 80%, with a $p < 0.05$ significance level and a moderate effect size. In selecting the desired level of differences between groups, remember that as the differences between groups increases, the power to detect these differences also increases.[9] Data from pilot studies or the literature is used in the calculation of the effect size or minimum difference between groups. It is often helpful when preparing a grant to include a table with the mean change following the same or a similar intervention and the effect size obtained to justify the chosen effect size. However, if these data are not available then you can select an appropriate sample size as defined by Cohen – small 0.20, moderate 0.50, large 0.80.[37] Remember that the sample size calculated is the best guess of the number of participants required to demonstrate a statistically significant difference – it is not a guarantee that that number is the true number. Providing the reviewers with sample size calculations for a range of effect sizes is also helpful to demonstrate the scope regarding the number of participants needed compared to the effect or difference achieved. When the primary endpoint is the occurrence of some event, as indicated above, the proportion of events in each groups is compared.[9] However, the variable of interest may be time to the event.[9] In this case, lifetable (tabular presentation of the total survival experience during the observation period) or survival analysis is the method of analysis and survival curves (graphical presentation of the total survival experience) for the groups are constructed.[9] For estimating the sample size using survival analysis, the assumptions employed in a commonly used model are that the survival curve follows an exponential distribution , where λ is called the hazard rate or force of mortality.[9] An estimate of λ is calculated as the inverse of the mean survival time or alternatively, the number of observed events divided by the total exposure time of the person at risk of the event.[9] Methods used for comparing survival curves include the proportional hazards model or the Cox regression model, Kaplan-Meier method, and the Cutler-Ederer method.[9]

Although as we discussed previously, covariance or stratified analysis adjusts the overall comparison of main outcomes for baseline variables, another approach is to analyze the intervention-control comparison within a subgroup of the sample such as male versus female or mild versus severe disease rather than or in addition to the overall comparison.[9] This is often done when there is the desire to isolate the characteristics of responders versus nonresponders or to identify those participants in whom the intervention is most beneficial.[9] As Friedman points out, the hope is to refine the primary hypothesis and specify to whom, if anyone, the intervention should be recommended.[9] It may be helpful, for example, to examine differences in baseline characteristics between dropped or disqualified patients and those who go on to complete the study to see if there was a predictive variable regarding study completion. In this case, this additional analysis should be taken into consideration when conducting the power analysis to provide sufficient power to obtain significance for the subgroup analyses, especially since performing additional tests can increase the chance of a Type-I error.[9]

NONADHERENCE

The aim of randomized clinical trials is the determination of whether an intervention is effective. This comparison is compromised when there is underutilization of the intervention in one or both treatment arms. Thus, optimal adherence to the intervention is critical to a successful trial and nonadherence leads to underestimating the therapeutic or toxic effects.[9] Indeed, in a recent meta-analysis of clinical trials designed to examine the impact of CPAP on mean blood pressure, Haentjens and colleagues found that the results would have been different if the participants had a higher overall level of disease severity.[38] For each 10-event increase in the apnea-hypopneas index at baseline, a 0.89 mmHg decrease in blood pressure from the reported results would have occurred. More impressive, however, was the finding that for each increased hour of CPAP use, there would have been a 1.38 further decrease in blood pressure demonstrating the important contribution of adherence to study results. There are several reasons participants do not adhere to study procedures, including: (a) side effects; (b) not willing to change behavior; (c) not understanding instructions; (d) lack of family support; and (e) a change of mind regarding participation.[9] Reasons for why patients with obstructive sleep apnea are nonadherent to CPAP treatment are discussed elsewhere (see Weaver, T. E. and R. R. Grunstein (2008). Adherence to continuous positive airway pressure therapy: the challenge to effective treatment." Proc Am Thorac Soc 5(2):173-8). Studies have documented that normalization of impairments in neurobehavior and daytime functioning is more likely to occur when nightly CPAP use is greater than 5 h.[39,40] Across RCTs, the demonstration of CPAP treatment as an efficacious intervention may have been compromised by the fact that the mean nightly duration of use in these investigations was only 4.46 h for active CPAP and 4.85 for sham-CPAP (placebo), below an effective duration of use.[41]

The field of sleep medicine is fortunate that, with regard to CPAP treatment, it has superb methods to objectively document adherence. Indeed, CPAP use can be documented using data obtained via smartcard, modem, or the World Wide Web. However, the task is more daunting in studies involving pharmaceutical agents. Self-report is unreliable no matter what intervention is being evaluated. Electronic pill caps, such as MEMS caps, are superior to pill counts. Physiologic drug levels provide more compelling evidence of adherence to the study regimen. Plans for optimizing adherence should be developed as part of the initial planning phase of the study.[9] The shorter the study duration and the less complicated the intervention, the better the chance that adherence will be maintained.[9] Additional factors include selection of participants, whether the participant has a thorough understanding of what is expected of them in the study, and whether the participant is truly willing to follow the treatment regimen.[9] These factors can be evaluated during a run-in prior to randomization as well as increasing the ability to identify and eliminate those who are likely to become poor adherers.[9] Nonadherence to the intervention also contributes to missing data.

MISSING DATA

Having missing data can truly undermine achieving study objectives. This can happen when participants are unable to provide necessary information, inadequate physical examinations or retrieval of information from the medical record, laboratory mishaps, carelessness in completing study forms and data entry.[9] Irretrievable missing data can be imputed using the mean of the group for that question or overall score to substitute for participant response. The best approach, however, is to include plans to prevent missing data when planning the study. Clear definitions of entry and diagnostic criteria and methodology are critical to assure adequate and consistent data collection.[9] These should be provided in a well developed manual of procedures.[9] This manual should provide details regarding "what," "when," "who," and "how."[9] Forms that are well-designed and clear will reduce variability and help eliminate missing or erroneous data.[9] For example, does the term "date" on a form mean the date the participant completed the form or the date the data was entered. Case report forms (CRF) are essential components of a well-designed study. CRFs should be developed for the collection of all outcome measures as well as participant demographics, medications, and medical history. Training of all staff and investigators should not only include review of study protocol, but also clear articulation of roles and expectations regarding the execution of those roles. One time training is not usually adequate to insure

Terry Weaver, PhD and Connie M. Ulrich, PhD

accurate implementation of the protocol. Plans for retraining should also be developed. Site visits provide a good opportunity to observe study implementation, including return demonstration of the protocol, execute retraining of study staff, and obtain missing data. The verification that data contained in the database matches the data obtained at the point of collection (source data verification) is the method that should be applied to identify missing or erroneous data and obtain the missing data or make the correction before data analysis. A plan for source data verification should be developed that specifies the point at which data is evaluated (e.g., 10, 25, 50, 75, 100% of participants randomized). Monitoring forms for source data verification should be developed as a method of data quality control. This would include tracking drug handling, calibration of devices, and laboratory tests.[9]

EARLY STUDY TERMINATION

There are several reasons for the early termination of a study. The two major reasons are greater than expected serious adverse effects in the intervention group or a subgroup and when it is clear that a statistically significant difference cannot be achieved at the end of the study.[9] Other reasons include greater-than-expected beneficial effects and unachievable correction of logistical or extensive data-quality problems.[9] Prior to the initiation of the study, the reasons for potential study termination should be clearly articulated. Evaluation of study progress is determined during an interim analysis where safety issues and the likelihood of achieving study goals are examined. As a statistical comparison of differences between the two groups may be done during an interim analysis, this should be considered when developing the statistical analysis plan and sample size as this analysis decreases the power of the study. That is, there is a reduction in study power with each "peak" of the data with regard to treatment comparison. This would not be a consideration if only study safety is reviewed and a statistical analysis comparing treatment arms is not conducted. The interim analysis is carried out by the DSMB and results of the statistical results with regard to alpha level obtained are not shared with blinded study personnel when the study is double-blinded. Often the DSMB is also blinded and the analysis is executed in a blinded fashion, that is, Treatment A is compared to Treatment B with the DSMB being blinded as to which is the active treatment. Several factors should be considered when determining whether a study should be terminated[9]:

a. Possible differences in prognostic factors between the two treatment groups at baseline
b. Potential bias in the assessment of response variables, especially when the study is not double-blinded
c. Possible impact of missing data should be evaluated
d. Differential concomitant intervention and levels of adherence should be considered for their impact on study results
e. Potential side effects and outcomes of secondary response variables
f. Internal consistency should be examined
g. The experience of the study groups over time in long-term trials
h. The outcomes of similar trials – new findings in the literature that would affect the outcomes or safety of the study
i. Impact of early termination on credibility and acceptability of the results

In summary, when conducting a RCT, there are several issues that should be addressed when selecting the design. Consideration should be given to the nature of the response variables, method of data collection and quality control, and training related to data collection, intervention delivery, and quality control. As discussed below, a termination policy including stopping rules should be articulated. Clinical trials, especially those that are multisite, are complex attention should be paid to the organization of the study team, the selection of participating sites, role of site investigators, data coordinating center, and overall study administration including identification of a Steering Committee, frequency of team meetings, and site visits.

SUMMARY

The key to a successful study is comprehensive planning that includes the selection of the appropriate design that will achieve study aims minimizes threats to validity and sources of error; plans for the protection of participants and the ethical conduct of the study; adequate determination of sample size to provide an adequately powered study with consideration of the potential number of drop outs; promotion of adherence to the intervention; detailed training plan; well-developed manual of procedures; approaches to prevent missing data and promoting data quality control; and clear articulation of the situations under which a study will be terminated.

REFERENCES

1. Abdi H. The Bonferonni and Šidák Corrections for Multiple Comparisons. In: Salkind N, ed. Encyclopedia of Measurement and Statistics. Thousand Oaks (CA): Sage; 2007.

2. Trochim WMK. Internal Validity. In: Web Center for Social Research Methods, ed. The Knowledge Base - Research Methods; vol 2006. http://www.socialresearchmethods.net/kb/intval.php, accessed 2009

3. What do Hawthorne and John Henry have in common? Siphoning Off a few Thoughts. vol; December 5, 2007. http://tukopamoja.wordpress.com/2007/12/05/what-do-hawthorne-and-john-henry-have-in-common/, accessed 2009.

4. Trochim WMK. Construct validity. In: Web Center for Social Research Methods, ed The Knowledge Base - Research Methods. vol; 2006. http://www.socialresearchmethods.net/kb/constval.php, accessed 2009.

5. Trochim WMK. Threats to construct validity. In: Web Center for Social Research Methods, ed The Knowledge Base - Research Methods. vol; 2006. http://www.socialresearchmethods.net/kb/consthre.php, accessed 2009.

6. Trochim WMK. External validity. In Web Center for Social Research Methods, ed The Knowledge Base - Research Methods.vol. 2006. http://www.socialresearchmethods.net/kb/external.php, accessed 2009.

7. Trochim WMK. Types of Survey. In Web Center for Social Research Methods, ed The Knowledge Base - Research Methods.vol; 2006. http://www.socialresearchmethods.net/kb/survtype.php, accessed 2009.

8. Trochim WMK. Selecting the survey method. In Web Center for Social Research Methods, ed The Knowledge Base - Research Methods.vol. 2006. http://www.socialresearchmethods.net/kb/survsel.php, accessed 2009.

9. Friedman L, Furberg C, DeMets D. Fundamentals of clinical trials. New York: Springer; 1998.

10. Permuted block design. *CONSORT.* Transparent reporting of trials. 2009 vol; 2007. http://www.consort-statement.org/resources/glossary/m---p/permuted-block-design/,accessed 2009.

11. Department of Health and Human Services. The Common Rule, Title 45 (Public Welfare). Code of Federal Regulations, Part 46 (Protection of Human Subjects): National Institutes of Health, Office for Human Research Protections; 2009. http://www.hhs.gov/ohrp/humansubjects/guidance/45cfr46.htm, accessed 2009

12. Levine R. The nature, scope, and justification of clinical research: What is research? Who is the subject? In: Emanuel E, Grady C, Crouch R, Lie R, Miller F, Wendler D, eds. The Oxford Textbook of Clinical Research Ethics. New York: Oxford University Press; 2008:211-21.

13. Emanuel EJ, Wendler D, Grady C. What makes clinical research ethical? JAMA 2000;283:2701-11.

14. Freedman B. Equipoise and the ethics of clinical research. N Engl J Med 1987;317:141-5.

15. Lilford RJ, Jackson J. Equipoise and the ethics of randomization. J R Soc Med 1995;88:552-9.

16. Miller FG, Brody H. Clinical equipoise and the incoherence of research ethics. J Med Philos 2007;32:151-65.

17. Miller FG, Brody H. A critique of clinical equipoise. Therapeutic misconception in the ethics of clinical trials. Hastings Cent Rep 2003;33:19-28.

Terry Weaver, PhD and Connie M. Ulrich, PhD

18. Joffe S, Truog R. Equipoise and randomization. In: Emanuel E, Grady C, Crouch R, Lie R, Miller F, Wendler D, eds. The Oxford Textbook of Clinical Research Ethics. New York: Oxford University Press; 2008:245-60.

19. Fried C. Medical Experimentation: Personal Integrity and Social Policy. Amsterdam: North-Holland Publishing; 1974.

20. Markman M. Ethical difficulties with randomized clinical trials involving cancer patients: examples from the field of gynecologic oncology. J Clin Ethics 1992;3:193-5.

21. Daugherty CK, Ratain MJ, Emanuel EJ et al. Ethical, scientific, and regulatory perspectives regarding the use of placebos in cancer clinical trials. J Clin Oncol 2008;26:1371-8.

22. The National Commission for the Protection of Human Subjects of Biomedical and Behavioral Research. The Belmont Report: Ethical Principles and Guidelines for the Protection of Human Subjects Research. Publication OS 78-0012. Department of Health and Education Welfare; 1978. http://www.hhs.gov/ohrp/humansubjects/guidance/belmont.html, accessed 2009

23. Castro M. Placebo versus best-available-therapy control group in clinical trials for pharmacologic therapies: which is better? Proc Am Thorac Soc 2007;4:570-3.

24. Shapiro AK. Factors Contributing to the Placebo Effect. Their Implications for Psychotherapy. Am J Psychother 1964;18:SUPPL 1:73-88.

25. Clark P, Leaverton P. Scientific and ethical issues in the use of placebo controls in clinical trials. Ann Rev PUblic Health 1994;5:19-38.

26. Piantodosi s. Clinical Trials: A Methodologic Perspective. New York: John Wiley & Sons; 1997.

27. World Medical Association. Declaration of Helsinki: Ethical Principles for Medical Research Involving Human Subjects. vol; 2004. http://www.wma.net/e/policy/b3.htm, accessed 2009.

28. Miller F. The ethics of placebo-controlled trials. In: Emanuel E, Grady C, Crouch R, Lie R, Miller F, Wendler D, eds. The Oxford Textbook of Clinical Research Ethics. New York: Oxford University Press; 2008:261-72.

29. Sutherland ER. Sham procedure versus usual care as the control in clinical trials of devices: which is better? Proc Am Thorac Soc 2007;4:574-6.

30. Miller FG, Kaptchuk TJ. Sham procedures and the ethics of clinical trials. J R Soc Med 2004;97:576-8.

31. Horng S, Miller FG. Ethical framework for the use of sham procedures in clinical trials. Crit Care Med 2003;31:S126-30.

32. Bedard PL, Krzyzanowska MK, Pintilie M et al. Statistical power of negative randomized controlled trials presented at American Society for Clinical Oncology annual meetings. J Clin Oncol 2007;25:3482-7.

33. Polit D, Hungler B. Nursing Research: Principles and Methods. 6 ed. Philadelphia: Lippincott, Williams & Wilkins; 1999.

34. Halpern SD, Karlawish JH, Berlin JA. The continuing unethical conduct of underpowered clinical trials. JAMA 2002;288:358-62.

35. Friedman L, Schron E. Data and safety monitoring boards. In: The nature s, and justification of clinical research: What is research? Who is the subject?, ed. The Oxford Textbook of Clinical Research Ethics. New York: Oxford University Press; 2008:569-76.

36. Spilker B. Guide to Clinical Trials. Philadelphia: Lippincott Williams & Wilkins; 1991.

37. Cohen J. Statistical Power Analysis for the Behavioral Sciences. Hillsdale: Lawrence Erlbaum Associates; 1988.

38. Haentjens P, Van Meerhaeghe A, Moscariello A et al. The impact of continuous positive airway pressure on blood pressure in patients with obstructive sleep apnea syndrome: evidence from a meta-analysis of placebo-controlled randomized trials. Arch Intern Med 2007;167:757-64.

39. Weaver TE, Maislin G, Dinges DF et al. Relationship between hours of CPAP use and achieving normal levels of sleepiness and daily functioning. Sleep 2007;30:711-9.

40. Zimmerman ME, Arnedt JT, Stanchina M et al. Normalization of memory performance and positive airway pressure adherence in memory-impaired patients with obstructive sleep apnea. Chest 2006;130:1772-8.

41. Gay P, Weaver T, Loube D et al. Evaluation of positive airway pressure treatment for sleep related breathing disorders in adults. Sleep 2006;29:381-401.

Chapter VI

Special Considerations for Animal and Translational Research

Seiji Nishino, MD, PhD

Introduction

Progress in understanding of basic sleep physiology largely owes to animal experiments in which various invasive techniques, such as *in vivo/in vitro* electrophysiology, brain lesion/transaction, and functional neurochemical/anatomical experiments, have been applied. Genetic engineering (gene targeting and transgenic) is also a powerful technique in basic sleep research using animals (see[1] for review).

Animal models of human diseases are also available for various sleep disorders that occur both spontaneously and when produced by genetic engineering or special manipulations such as light phase sift and exposures to stress environment. As an example, consider sleep. *The International Classification of Sleep Disorders* (*ICSD-2*) lists over 84 different types of sleep disorders.[2] Different pathophysiological/etiological mechanisms likely exist for each sleep disorder, but the etiology of most sleep disorders is largely unknown.

Continuing with this example, research using validated animal models of sleep disorders may lead to a breakthrough for understanding the etiology and pathophysiology of the human disease. A good example is the success of research using animal models of narcolepsy. With both forward genetic (in familial narcoleptic dogs) and reverse genetic approaches (in orexin/hypocretin gene knockout [KO] mice), genes responsible for narcolepsy in dogs and mice have been identified.[3,4] Subsequently, it has been found that the same deficiency found in the neurotransmitter system (hypocretin/orexin) of the animal models is indeed involved in human narcolepsy,[5,6] stressing the value of use of validated animal models for sleep research. These animal models are also very valuable for developing new treatments for human sleep disorders, and these experiments are in progress (see[7] for review).

Some physiological and pathophysiological aspects of sleep mechanisms can also be investigated in much simpler animals such as zebra fishes or fruit flies, with various molecular and genetic approaches.

All medical research must be carefully planned, and animal research is no exception. Experts who review a scientist's proposed experiment involving animals weigh several considerations before approving each study. First of all, the research must be relevant to human or animal health, and all studies must protect the animals' welfare. Under federal law, all animals must be treated humanely and undergo the least distress possible. These considerations must be made for scientific grant submissions. For the National Institutes of Health (NIH) research grant submission, the study sections review the Vertebrae Animal Section (VAS), and any concerns by the reviewers and NIH officers will be cited in the summary statement. These concerns should be resolved and the applicants are given the opportunity to answer concerns prior to the award.

The following items in **Table 1** are considered for the review of the VAS associated with the NIH grant submission, and all applicants should be aware of all requirements.

In this chapter, Special Considerations for Animal and Translational Research in sleep research especially required for the grant submissions are discussed.

*The Institute for Laboratory Animal Research (ILAR) published the two reports approved by the Governing Board of the National Research Council, "Guide for the Care and Use of Laboratory Animals"[9] and "Guidelines for the Use of Animals in Neuroscience and Behavioral Research."[10] These guidelines are comprehensive and useful for all researchers using animals. Some portions of the contents of this chapter are from these two guidelines. Some specific information, such as suggested dosage for anesthesia and analgesia are from the Institutional Animal Care and Use Committee (IACUC) at Stanford University (i.e., Administrative Panel on Laboratory Animal Care [APLAC]), and the Web site links for these sources are provided in **Table 4** on Page 73.*

Table 1   Checklist for Review of Vertebrate Animal Section (VAS)[8]

1. Description of animals and their use: Address for all species proposed.
- ✓ Species
- ✓ Strain
- ✓ Ages
- ✓ Sex
- ✓ Number of animals to be used
- ✓ Concise, but complete description of procedures; sufficient information for evaluation

2. Justification for:
- ✓ The use of animals
- ✓ Choice of species
- ✓ For non-human primates (NHP), dogs or cats, additional justification is provided
- ✓ Number of animals to be used (power calculations cited if appropriate)

3. Veterinary care (for all colloboration site):
- ✓ Availability of veterinary care
- ✓ How often animals are monitored for health by veterinary or animal care staff
- ✓ How monitoring occurs during anesthesia and recovery (if applicable)
- ✓ When and how veterinary staff communicate with the investigator
- ✓ Indicators for veterinary intervention
- ✓ Description of intervention procedures by veterinary staff (if indicated)

4. Provisions to minimize discomfort, distress, pain and injury:
- ✓ Procedures and circumstances are identified when discomfort, distress, pain or injury may occur
- ✓ Tranquilizers, analgesics, anesthetics, and other treatments are identified by name and their use described
- ✓ Care, monitoring, or special housing (if indicated) following surgery or procedures
- ✓ If survival surgery is proposed, anesthesia, post-surgical analgesia and other treatments (if indicated) are described
- ✓ Indicators of humane endpoints
- ✓ Brief description of restraint devices, if relevant

5. Euthanasia:
- ✓ Method(s) for euthanasia and reasons for selection(s)
- ✓ Stated that method is consistent with AVMA Guidelines on Euthanasia
- ✓ Scientific justification for choice of method if not AVMA recommended

Applicant responsibilities
Each of the five points must be addressed in the VAS of NIH applications or proposals. All of the items must be complete and evaluated by reviewers as appropriate for an application to be ACCEPTABLE.

CONSIDERATIONS IN THE SELECTION OF ANIMAL SPECIES AND MODELS

Selection of the animal species is one of the most important issues for animal research, and basic sleep research is no exception. The selection of the species may depend on the experimental setting and the regulations/restrictions of the institute's animal facilities. The budgetary/funding situations also influence the selection. If the animal models for sleep disorders of interest have already been established and validated in certain animal species, there is an advantage in using these models. In any case, the justifications for the choice of animal species need to be noted when you submit the research grant proposals. There are also several important issues, especially when pharmacological studies are planned for the animals. These may also affect the selection of the animal species, thus should also be discussed.

Primates, dogs, cats, rodents (rats and mice), and some simpler animals such as fruit flies or zebra fishes, are probably the major animal species considered for research. To illustrate this point, some of the important characteristics of theses species in sleep research are summarized in **Table 2**.

In the following paragraphs, I will use the sleep field to illustrate the role of animal models in research.

The cyclical organization of sleep varies between species, and the period length of each sleep cycle increases with brain size across species.[11] In adult humans and non-human primates, the circadian distribution of sleep tends to be monophasic, whereas it is polyphasic in the rat, mouse, and cat. Human non-rapid eye movement (NREM) sleep and rapid eye movement (REM) sleep alternate throughout the 4–6 sleep cycles occurring every night, while in the rat, mouse, and cat, NREM–REM cycles are much shorter. In these species, the cyclic NREM–REM sleep epochs continue throughout sleep during the day and night, except when they are engaged in other activities requiring wakefulness. Given this clear difference of sleep architecture in human and rodents, it is reasonable to assume that the characteristics of sleep abnormalities should somewhat differ. Nevertheless, the main homeostatic, circadian, and neurochemical modulations of sleep remain essentially similar between species,[12] suggesting that sleep regulations in human and other animal species also share common underlying mechanisms.

Historically, dogs and cats had been frequently used for sleep research. One of the reasons for this is that sleep electroencephalographic (EEG) patterns of these species are similar to that of human, and more sleep stages (drowsy, light sleep and deep sleep, in addition to slow wave sleep [SWS] and REM sleep) can be distinguished in these species. Sleep is more consolidated compared to that of rodents. Cats have often been used for *in vivo* electrophysiological studies (they sleep well with the head fixed in the recording device) and brain transduction studies, but it is now difficult to obtain the animal (mostly from class B breeders, but this is not recommended, especially for long-term study by most animal facilities). Many investigators now use rodents for *in vivo* electrophysiological experiments, and the need for using cats for sleep research is now limited. Due to the existence of spontaneously occurring narcolepsy in dogs, they have also been intensively used for basic sleep research (*in vivo* electrophysiological and microdialysis and pharmacological experiments).[1] Since familial narcoleptic dogs (that can be produced in the breeding colony) were found to be caused by the hypocretin receptor mutation which is dissimilar to the etiology of human narcolepsy, the value of the familial canine narcoleptic model diminished, and most of the experiments are taken over by those using rodent models of narcolepsy.

Rats and mice are thus the most popular animal species used for basic sleep research. The research methods in these species include, *in vivo* sleep assay combined with physiological and pharmacological experiments, *in vivo* and *in vitro* electrophysiology and neurochemical and neuroanatomical experiments. The experiments using these species are cost efficient by means of housing space/cost and the large number of animals can be rapidly reproduced within the breeding colony. In comparison to mice, rats may be better suited for sleep research because their larger size facilitates experimental manipulation.

It should be noted that rodents are nocturnal animals, and thus need special attention: melatonin does not promote sleep, and light exposure produces immediate and significant behavioral sedation. They can be stressed in new environments (even by new clean cages), and investigators use this characteristic to produce rodent insomnia models.[13]

One of the foremost merits using the rodents, especially mice, is that the genetically modified animals are readily available for the experiments. This includes gene targeting knockout mice, transgenic mice/rats,

Seiji Nishino, MD, PhD

antisense, and gene knockdown with RNA interferences. Random mutagenesis, with N-ethyl-N-nitrosurea (ENU), typically used for the simpler animals, is also applicable to mice. This method lead to the identification and cloning of the clock genes in mammals, one of the most important discoveries in neuroscience in the 20th century.[14] These discoveries lead to the understanding of the molecular mechanisms involved in the circadian clock of mammals.[15,16] As mentioned before, recombinant gene KO mice (preprohypocretin/preproorexin gene KO) significantly contributed to the progress in narcolepsy research in humans. This evidence proves the usefulness of genetically modified mice in sleep research.

Since research using genetically modified animals is one of most popular methods in basic sleep research and this is also tightly connected with the selection of the animal species, important characteristics of each approach are briefly described.

GENE TARGETING AND GENETICALLY MODIFIED ANIMALS

Random Mutagenesis

The mutagenesis approach is straightforward: mutation occurs at random in the whole genome; this is followed by high throughput screening of all mutant offspring to detect a major effect on a given phenotype. Both dominant and recessive mutations can be screened in the same way as a single gene mutation in a pathological condition. This approach has been used in sleep and behavioral neuroscience in mice, fruit fly and zebra fish. Once the mutated gene is localized, candidate gene or positional cloning approaches are used for its identification, and ultimately its functional analysis can be performed by gain or loss of function. Thus, it is likely that this approach may also be useful in generating a number of "sleep" mutants. However, there are also some drawbacks for this approach; genetic screens may not be able to identify small-effect sequence variations that may turn out to be essential for some aspects of the phenotype. In addition, with currently available technologies, recording and analyzing sleep of thousands of mice in a mutant screen does not seem feasible, at least not in a single academic laboratory, but this may not be a concern for research in simpler animals.

Sleep Phenotype Variations and QTL

The quantitative trait loci (QTL) method is one of the genome-wide approaches used to detect all genes with variable effects on the trait, and it has been extensively used to analyze natural polygenic traits in mice (see, for example, reference[17]). A significant phenotypic variability of sleep observed between different inbred mice strains[18,19] suggested complex interactions between a number of genes.

QTL analysis was therefore applied in various inbred mice to dissect sleep related genes. Quantitative analyses of EEG power spectra also showed that sleep EEG components differ significantly between different inbred strains of mice.[18] The homeostatic drive, which is related to the duration of prior wakefulness,[20] is also strongly influenced by the genotype of the mouse.[18] Thus, delta power rebound after sleep deprivation in B6xD2 recombinant inbred strains was used in QTL analyses to map genes underlying this phenotype.[18] A significant QTL (named delta power in slow-wave sleep or Dps1) was identified on chromosome 13 that was responsible for 50% of the genetic variance in this trait.[18] Subsequent experiments by examining the expression pattern of selected genes located in the Dps1 interval, in sleep and wakefulness, in B6 and D2 parental strains, identified the strongest candidate gene *Homer1a*.[21,22] Although the candidate gene identified by the QTL must be mutated either by classical homologous recombination (knock-out) or by the serial nested chromosomal deletions to examine if the identified genes are indeed responsible for the observed phenotype variations, this may be the first sleep regulatory gene identified by the QTL.

Candidate Gene Approaches, Transgenic, Gene Knockout, Knock-In and Knockdown

As opposed to the classical forward genetic approaches to find genes involved in genetic diseases, reverse genetic approaches evaluate influences of alteration of known genes in the expression of a trait of interest. Reverse genetics have been made possible by the development of gene targeting and transgenic animals. By homologues recombination in embryonic stem cells, an altered gene construct can replace the existing gene.[23] If the inserted gene-construct translates into a nonfunctional protein, the animals homozygous for this construct are often referred to as "knock-out" animals. With non-homologues (illegitimate) recombination one or more gene copies are inserted into the genome at undefined locations.[24] Animals carrying these constructs are often referred to as transgenic animals. Animals produced with this transgenic method often are gain-of-function mutants since they express a novel gene product or over express a normal gene. With both techniques, one can create animal models to study the effects of change in protein levels on sleep (from over expression in transgenics, to nonfunctional protein in knock-outs) and altered or novel proteins (knock-in and transgenic). These animal models are also useful in confirming the role of genes that were identified by forward genetic approaches (see[25]).

Since large numbers of knock-out and transgenic mice have been used in the sleep research field, this chapter does not cover the findings from these mice, but a summary table is available in the review articles[1].

Although knock-out rats are not yet available, Beuckman and colleagues produced narcoleptic transgenic rats carrying the promoter of the human prepro-orexin gene ligated to a truncated human ataxin-3.[26] Similar to the results reported in orexin/ataxin-3 narcoleptic mice,[7] rats exhibit cataplexy-like behavior and fragmented vigilance states, a decreased latency to rapid REM sleep and direct transitions from wakefulness to REM sleep, suggesting hypocretin/ataxin-3 transgenic rats could provide a useful model of human narcolepsy. The usefulness of the rat as a model system has been strengthened by rapid progress of the Rat Genome Project, which has a goal of identifying unique rat genes by extensive mapping efforts, as well as availability of numerous inbred and recombinant rat strains.[8] Similarly, rat pluripotent embryonic stem cells, capable of producing chimera rats, have been recently established,[9] and thus basic research using genetically altered rats are of great potential and promise in the future of sleep research.

General Considerations for Interpreting the Results Using Knock-Out and Transgenic Mice

The considerations and limitations of these approaches should also be discussed. Genetic background can significantly affect behavioral measures. The majority of knock-out mice are crosses between the 129SV strain used to obtain embryonic stem cells and different inbred mouse strains. As explained in the QTL section, sleep phenotypes significantly vary among mice with different genetic backgrounds. Therefore, it is possible that genetic background segregates in mutants independently of the mutation itself, and the behavioral data must be interpreted cautiously.[30] Most researchers are now aware of this concern, but it still takes a long time to generate the congenic mice line to match the genetic background between knock-out and wild type mice.

Sleep is fundamentally physiological and is essential for survival, and multiple systems are involved in its regulation. Therefore if the congenital knock-out/trangenic mice do not develop lethal phenotypes, developmental compensation (e.g., other molecules could compensate for the lacking protein[25]) are likely to have occurred. Some of these issues could be overcome by developing (tissue-specific) conditional or inducible knock-out models where the acute effects of loss-of-function can be studied in structures of interest.[31] There are several advantages conferred by conditioned knockout over the conventional type in that such genetically modified mice are not only able to survive longer but also, the technique overall is more "clean" and "scientifically precise." The most commonly used technique for conditional gene knockout is the Cre-loxP recombinase system. Cre recombinase is used to delete a segment of DNA flanked

Seiji Nishino, MD, PhD

by LoxP sites in an experimental animal.[32] It has been used to generate animals with mutations limited to certain cell types (tissue-specific knockout) or animals with mutations that can be activated by drug administration (inducible knockout) in a number of transgenic species. The availability of transgenic lines with tissue specific or inducible Cre expression also permits researchers to inactivate or activate a gene of interest simply by breeding a floxed animal to pre-existing Cre-transgenics.

Antisense Targeting and Gene Knockdown

Another strategy that qualifies as a reverse genetic strategy is antisense targeting. With this strategy one can selectively, locally, and transiently down-regulate the expression of a gene product at the level of the RNA or DNA.[33] The basic idea is to induce translational arrest through sequence specific hybridization of the mRNA to synthetic oligodeoxynucletides. This technique has been applied to study the effects on sleep of c-Fos protein expression in the medial pre-optic area,[34] of glutamic-acid decarboxylase,[35] and hypocretin-2 receptor.[36] This approach can be applied to both mice and rats, and the sequence information of genes of interests becomes available.

In addition to antisense targeting, the RNA interference pathway is often exploited in experimental biology to study the function of genes in cell culture and *in vivo* in model organisms.[37] Double-stranded RNA is synthesized with a sequence complementary to a gene of interest and introduced into a cell or organism, where it is recognized as exogenous genetic material and activates the RNAi pathway. Using this mechanism, researchers can cause a drastic decrease (knockdown) in the expression of a targeted gene, and this technique is also useful for basic sleep research.

SIMPLER ANIMAL MODELS

Molecular biology and other technical advances are most efficiently applied to large numbers of rapidly reproducing, inexpensive, small organisms, including prokaryotes and invertebrates as well as simple vertebrates, to study complex behaviors, such as circadian rhythms and long-term memory consolidation. Furthermore, the information gained can often be shown to be relevant to humans by demonstrating that the genes and their products are evolutionarily conserved (see a review by[38]).

In 1984, Campbell and Tobler reviewed over 100 studies in over 150 species seeking evidence for sleep from invertebrates to primates, using behavioral criteria. The behaviors required were: (a) a stereotypic or species-specific posture; (b) behavioral quiescence; (c) an elevated arousal threshold; and (d) state reversibility with stimulation.[39] Using these criteria to review previous laboratory and field studies, the authors concluded that there is evidence for sleep-like states in 19 species of fish, 16 reptiles, and nine amphibians, as well as several invertebrates (cockroaches, bees, and octopi). Hendricks et al.[38] had augmented Tobler's criteria by explicitly stating and clarifying some features of "sleep" that seem intuitive, and they included a requirement for state-related neural functional changes. The neural changes need not resemble the specific state-related EEG patterns used to characterize mammalian and avian sleep. In simple animals, molecular or neurochemical techniques might be more suitable than electrophysiology in some systems to provide evidence that neuronal activity is altered in a state-related fashion.[38]

The candidate species for basic sleep research should be a common, inexpensive, plentiful animal. In addition, it would be ideal if sufficient molecular genetics information were readily available. An accessible central nervous system with anatomical analogies to the mammalian system would be helpful in allowing extrapolation to mammals. Sleep studies in Drosophila melanogaster (invertebrates) and Danio rerio (vertebrates) have been initiated by several authors, and some characteristics of these species in basic sleep research is listed in **Table 2**.

Table 2 Common Animal Species Used in Sleep Research

Species	Physiology (Sleep/EEG Patterns)	Pharmacology	Genetic Engineering	Notes	References
Mammals					
Primates	consolidated sleep/wake pattern, similar to human	predictive of human pharmacology	Gene targeting (antisense, gene therapy)	the most strictly regulated	
Dogs	less consolidated, sleep EEG similar to human	Diazepam does not induce sleep	Gene targeting (antisense, gene therapy)	strictly regulated	
Cats	less consolidated, sleep EEG similar to human	Diazepam does not induce sleep	Gene targeting (antisense, gene therapy)	difficult to obtain, difficult to maintain breeding colony	
Rats	*nocturnal, non-REM/REM	**Pharmacology; requires larger doses	Transgenic. ES cells are established (for knock out), gene targeting	most popular in sleep research	
Mice	*nocturnal, non-REM/REM	**Pharmacology; requires larger doses	Transgenic, knockout (congenital and conditioned), gene targeting	most popular in sleep research	
Simpler Animals					
Fruit fly	rest/activity pattern CNS local field potentials distinguishes rest/activity pattern	The CNS lacks anatomical structures analogous to those of mammals. Many of the neurotransmitters, receptors, and transport systems are evolutionarily conserved, including most of those related to sleep control in mammals: serotonin, dopamine, histamine, and acetylcholine.	Transgenic, mutagenesis, gene targeting	small size, prolific reproduction rates, small gene number, short life cycle, high throughput, automatic infrared monitoring system	75 76
Zebra fish	rest/activity pattern	Systematic drug administration can be done with bat application. Larval zebra fish is transparent, permitting direct visualization of the CNS. The piscine nervous system has considerable analogy to the mammalian regarding brainstem systems implicated in vigilance control.	Transgenic, mutagenesis, gene targeting	small size, prolific reproduction rates, the genetic data base lags behind that of Drosophila	77 78

*Melatonin does not promote sleep in nocturnal animal species
**Requires larger doses for compounds metabolized in the liver

Seiji Nishino, MD, PhD

EXISTING ANIMAL MODELS OF SLEEP DISORDERS

There are some well-established or popular animal models of human sleep disorders and this information is also useful to evaluate if the selection of the animal species and the model is compelling (Table 3). Most of animal models (except genetic narcolepsy models) are spontaneously occurring and are under the influence of multiple factors (polygenic transmissions and environmental factors), and disease heterogeneity is also suggested in many cases. This situation mirrors with that of the human disease, and the pathophysiology of these existing models may be more close to those of human disorders.

The lack of suitable animals models for insomnia, sleep apnea and restless legs syndrome/periodic leg movement during sleep (RLS/PLMS) have been emphasized, but several animal models of these conditions were introduced recently.

There are several rodent models of insomnia, including stress related models, genetic models, and modification of the light-dark cycles and circadian perturbations, and an extensive review article is available (see[13] for review).

Since prevalence of many sleep disorders such as insomnia and RLS/PLMS increases with aging, aged animals are often used for some sleep studies.[40]

Rat models of chronic intermittent hypoxia induced by modifying the composition of the breathing gas have also been used to investigate the effects of periodic oxygen desaturation in causing arousal.[41-43] This model is rather a model for the consequence of the hypoxia (and not one for the cause of the disease), but it has potential importance. Repetitive apneic events disrupt the normal physiologic interactions between sleep and other systems (e.g., increased sympathetic activation, vascular endothelial dysfunction, increased oxidative stress, inflammation, increased platelet aggregability, metabolic dysregulation) and the research using the validated animal models are essential for understanding these comorbidities.

STUDY DESIGN

Studies using animals should protect the animals' welfare, and under US Government Principlesk,[44] investigators should use the minimum number of animals required to obtain valid results. However, investigators frequently err on the side of using too few animals rather than too many.[45] That results in a study that has too little power to detect a meaningful or biologically significant result (i.e. Type II error). To avoid this error, researchers should calculate the sample size necessary to detect a statistically significant effect. Several factors must be known or estimated to calculate sample size[45]:

1. the size of the effect under study (difference between experimental groups)
2. the population standard deviation of the effect
3. the desired power of the experiment to detect the effect (usually 80-90%)
4. the significance level (usually 0.05 or 0.01).

In general, the smaller the effect size or the larger the population variability, the larger the sample size must be to detect a difference, and therefore results from pilot experiments are required to calculate the power. It should also be noted that using a more sophisticated experimental design and statistical analysis provides more power to detect an effect. Methods for computing sample size are described in[45] and.[10] This resource also refers to other useful resources listed in Table 3.

Some aspects of estimates (such as developing and producing genetically modified animals) particularly lead to difficulties in estimating the number of animals necessary for a given experiment. These are under influence of multiple factors, such as reproduction and survival rate that are often genotype specific. Since

Table 3 Animal Models of Sleep Disorders

Sleep Disorders	Species	Condition	Etiology/ Pathophysiology	Notes	References
Narcolepsy	Dog	Familial narcolepsy	hypocretin receptor 2 mutation	no hypocretin receptor 2 mutation in human	64 3
		Sporadic narcolepsy	hypocretin ligand deficiency, post natal cell death	condition similar to human cases no breeding colony	64
	Rat	hypocretin cell ablated narcolepsy	postnatal hypocretin cell death	condition similar to human cases	26
	Mouse	hypocretin KO		hypocretin cells remaining	4
		hypocretin cell ablated narcolepsy	postnatal hypocretin cell death	condition similar to human cases	27
Insomnia	Rat/ Mouse	Stress induced insomnia new environment psychological stress foot shock fear and fear conditioned stress			13 65
	Rat	VLPO lesions			66
Sleep apnea	English Bulldog	OSA (spontaneous)			67
	Dog	Isocapnic progressive hypoxia	Manipulated		68
	Rat	Chronic intermittent hypoxia	Manipulated		41 42 43
	Rat/ Mouse	Central apnea (spontaneous)			69 70
RBD	Dog	spontaneous			71
	Cat	spontaneous			71
PLMS	Dog	Narcoleptic Dobermans exhibit PLMS-like movements		increase in PLMS (but not RLS) in human narcolepsy	72
PLMS/RLS	Aged Rat				73
RLS	Rat	6-OHDA lesioned rats	Brain lesion		74
RLS	Mouse	6-OHDA lesioned and iron-deficient mice	Brain lesion/iron deficiency		74
PLMS	Mouse	Dopamine D3 receptor knockout mice			74

VLPO, ventrolateral preoptic area; OSA, obstructive sleep apnea; RBD, REM sleep behavior diosrder; PLMS, periodic limb movements in sleep; RLS, restless legs syndrome; 6-OHDA, 6-Hydroxydopamine

Seiji Nishino, MD, PhD

this estimation is critical for the grant applications, specifically for the budget and timeline estimation, the estimate should be made carefully based on all information available.

As described above, the age of the animals is an important factor since many sleep disorders such as insomnia and PLM/RLS increase with age, and justification for the age of animals should be made.

Most investigators use male animals for study, since it is known that menstrual and reproduction cycles affect sleep in female animals. The gender of animals used also needs to be justified.

As discussed in the QTL and KO mice section, the strain difference in sleep patterns is well known in mice (as well as in rat strains) and thus, justifications of the selection of the strain also needs to be made.

Sleep evaluation may need headstage/transmitter implantations, multiple surgeries and special restrictions, such as sleep deprivation, may also be needed. Therefore special care should be made at the time of study design of the sleep study, and this will be discussed below in the section for the Procedural Considerations.

Since sleep is easily influenced by the any health conditions, allowing appropriate recovery period from the surgeries and a sufficient acclamation to recording conditions are required before initiating sleep recordings.

For some special occasions, manipulation free animals will always need to be used (i.e. the same animals can not be used repeatedly). Some of the examples are the stress exposures and stimulant medications, since sensitizations or relapses often occur by repeated applications of the same manipulations/same drug administrations.

For pharmacological experiments, an appropriate wash out period (i.e., such as four times longer than the half-life of the compound) need to be employed to avoid the carrying over effects.

In any cases, the study design should be approved by the IACUC. The institutes that fund the research will request a copy of the approval of the animal protocol by the IACUC prior to giving the award.

BIOSAFETY AND GUIDELINES

There are many useful resources regarding Guidelines for Biosafety of Animal Research that can be found online, and the list is shown in **Table 4**. In this section, the principal of the Biosafety of Animal Research is descried.

All animal care and use programs should have an occupational health and safety program available to the staff. The animal care and use program must comply with federal, state, and local regulations, to ensure a safe and healthy workplace, and, naturally, it will depend on the facility, research activities, hazards, and animal species involved. The National Research Council has a publication, "Occupational Health and Safety in the Care and Use of Research Animals" that contains guidelines and references for establishing and maintaining an effective, comprehensive program (see **Table 4** for the link). Strong administrative support and a collaborative effort among different institutional functions, such as the research program (as represented by the investigator), the animal care and use program (as represented by the veterinarian and the IACUC), the environmental health and safety program, occupational health services, and administration (e.g., human resources, finance, and facility-maintenance personnel), are essential for an effective health and safety program. However operational and day-to-day responsibility for safety in the workplace is on the laboratory or facility supervisor (e.g., principal investigator, facility director, or veterinarian) and also depends on the safe work practices of all employees. Hazard identification and risk assessment professional staff who conduct and support research programs involving hazardous biologic, chemical, or physical agents, should be qualified to

Table 4 Useful Resources and Online Links

OACU and OLAW

The Office of Animal Care and Use (OACU)	http://oacu.od.nih.gov/training/index.htm
Office of Laboratory Animal Welfare (OLAW)	http://grants.nih.gov/grants/olaw/olaw.htm

Guidelines

Guide for the Care and Use of Laboratory Animals (1996) Institute for Laboratory Animal Research (ILAR)	http://www.nap.edu/openbook.php?record_id=5140
Guidelines for the Care and Use of Mammals in Neuroscience and Behavioral Research, 2003 Institute for Laboratory Animal Research (ILAR)	http://grants.nih.gov/grants/olaw/National_Academies_ Guidelines_for_Use_and_Care.pdf
Occupational Health and Safety in the Care and Use of Research Animals The National Research Council	http://www.nap.edu/openbook.php?isbn=0309052998
AVMA Guidelines on Euthanasia	http://www.avma.org/issues/animal_welfare/euthanasia.pdf
Animal Species Used in Research The Humane Society of the United States	http://www.hsus.org/animals_in_research/ species_used_in_research/

Grant Writing Tips

How to Write an Application Involving Research Animals National Institute of Allergy and Infectious Diseases (NIAID)	http://www.niaid.nih.gov/ncn/clinical/researchanimals/ tutorial/index.htm

Selected Information from the Stanford Comparative Medicine Web site

Get Help Completing Research Plan Section F, Vertebrate Animals	http://med.stanford.edu/compmed/research/grants.html http://med.stanford.edu/compmed/docs/Grant_Writing_ Tips.pdf
Anesthesia and Analgesia	http://med.stanford.edu/compmed/animal_care/ guidelines.html

assess dangers associated with these programs and to select safeguards appropriate for each risk. An effective occupational health and safety program would be one that ensures that the risks associated with the experimental use of animals are reduced to acceptable levels. Potential hazards-such as animal bites, chemical cleaning agents, allergens, and zoonoses that are inherent in or intrinsic to animal use should also be identified and evaluated. Health and safety specialists with knowledge in appropriate disciplines should be involved in the assessment of risks associated with hazardous activities and in the development of procedures to manage such risks.

Training for zoonoses, chemical safety, microbiologic and physical hazards (including those related to radiation and allergies), unusual conditions or agents that might be part of experimental procedures (including the use of genetically engineered animals and the use of human tissue in immunocompromised animals), waste materials handeling, personal hygiene, and other considerations (e.g., precautions to be taken during personnel pregnancy, illness, or decreased immunocompetence) should be provided to personnel depending on which risk they are exposed to in their workplace.

Exposure to anesthetic gases (e.g., isoflurane, halothane) can cause adverse health effects. These include behavioral modification, physical impairment, or headaches from exposure to sub-anesthetic concentrations,

Seiji Nishino, MD, PhD

as well as reproductive or hepatotoxic effects from chronic exposure. Working in a vented fume hood or use of proper gas delivery (i.e., precision vaporizer) and scavenging equipment (e.g., F-Air charcoal canister) dramatically reduce risk of exposure.

ANIMAL FACILITY AND VETERINARY CARE ISSUES

Guidelines for Animal Facility and Veterinary Care Issues are also available online, and, thus, these issues are briefly discussed. Information for Animal Facility and Veterinary Care issues need to be provided to the reviewer and funding agencies, and the information needs to convince reviewers that you have the equipment, space, staff, and facilities to conduct the research, including essential resources such as Animal Facilities. The Stanford University Comparative Medicine Web site provides an example of how to fill the Resources (Animal Facilities) section of the NIH grant application (see Table 4).

ANIMAL ENVIRONMENT

Proper housing and management of animal facilities are essential to animal well-being, to the quality of research data and teaching or testing programs in which animals are used, and to the health and safety of personnel. Management programs should provide the environment, housing, and care that allow growth, maturing, reproduction, and maintenance of good health of the animal. It promotes animal well-being, and minimizes variations that can affect research results. The specific operating practices will depend on many factors unique to individual institutions and situations, but well-trained and motivated staff can often ensure high-quality animal care, even in institutions with less than optimal physical plants or equipment.

Many factors need to be taken into consideration to find adequate and appropriate physical and social environment, housing, space, and management.

The ILAR guide[9] lists the following factors:

a. The species, strain, and breed of the animal and individual characteristics, such as sex, age, size, behavior, experiences, and health.
b. The ability of the animals to form social groups with conspecifics through sight, smell, and possibly contact, whether the animals are maintained singly or in groups.
c. The design and construction of housing.
d. The availability or suitability of enrichments.
e. The project goals and experimental design (e.g., production, breeding, research, testing, and teaching).
f. The intensity of animal manipulation and invasiveness of the procedures conducted.
g. The presence of hazardous or disease-causing materials.
h. The duration of the holding period.

Animals should be housed to maximize species-specific behaviors and minimize stress-induced behaviors. Social species such as primates and dogs normally require housing in compatible pairs or groups. Animal care personnel should develop strategies for desired housing, which need to be reviewed and approved by the IACUC. Decisions by the IACUC are made while consulting the investigator and veterinarian, and should aim for high standards for professional and husbandry practices. It should be appropriate for the health and well-being of the species and consistent with research objectives. After the decision-making, objective assessments should be made to substantiate the adequacy of animal environment, husbandry, and management.

The environment in which animals are maintained should be appropriate for the species, its life history, and its intended use. For some species, simulating a natural environment might be appropriate for breeding and maintenance. Expert advice may be sought for special requirements associated with a certain experiment or animal subject (e.g., hazardous-agent use, behavioral studies, immunocompromised animals, farm animals, and nontraditional laboratory species).

VETERINARY CARE

Adequate veterinary care is required, including evaluation of health/well-being of all animals. Programmatic needs (institutional mission, programmatic goals, size of the animal program) will determine the need for full-time, part-time, or consultative veterinary services and the appropriate visit intervals for the case of part-time services.

Ethical, humane, and scientific considerations sometimes require the use of sedatives, analgesics, or anesthetics in animals (see the section below). An attending veterinarian should advise the research personnel so that humane needs are met and protocols are compatible with scientific requirements. The Animal Welfare Regulations[46] and Public Health Service Policy on Humane Care and Use of Laboratory Animals[47] require the attending veterinarian to have the authority to oversee the adequacy of other aspects of animal care and use, including animal husbandry and nutrition, sanitation practices, zoonosis control, and hazard containment.

MONITORING PROCEDURES

Animals must be monitored twice daily, in the early morning and late afternoon, including weekends and holidays. Any animals displaying clinically abnormal behavior must be removed from group housing situations to individual housing where food and water are easily accessible.

Time and person conducting the observation, observations such as the number of animals evidencing clinically abnormal behavior and the number of animals found dead should be recorded in writing for all monitoring sessions.

Animal behavior can be an excellent measure for assessing overall health. The clinical signs used to diagnose disease in animals are often based on behavior (for example, signs of pain). Thus, for assessment of animal health, the veterinarian or other professional should have a clear understanding of animal behavior. The American Veterinary Medical Association formally recognized the importance of animal behavior in relation to its health and to the veterinary profession in 1993 when it gave the American College of Veterinary Behaviorists (ACVB) specialty-board status. In the research environment, routine behavioral observations can be used to screen for diseases in animals with no clinical signs. Food or fluid intake and performance of specific tasks are some of the sensitive indicators of the animal's health condition.[48] Neuroscientists can readily monitor animal behavior and health because of several reasons: neuroscience and behavioral studies use individual animals for a relatively long term, the researcher is in close contact with the animal, and various behavioral data are collected during a study, such as locomotor and body temperature. As stated before, sleep is easy influenced by any other physical conditions. However, sleep may not be suitable for daily health monitoring since most of researchers do not analyze sleep real time and there is a time lag between data acquisition and analysis. Thus, subtle changes in the animal's demeanor, its willingness to work in a study, or sudden changes in performance on behavioral tasks may be the first indicators of a health problem. Researchers should promptly notify such changes to the veterinarian for full evaluation of animal health.

MONITORING THE SITE SURROUNDING AN IMPLANTED DEVICE

As an example, sleep recordings require headstage (or telemetry devices) and electrode implantation, which requires special care. Sites surrounding implanted devices or hardware, such as electroencephalogram

(EEG) and electromyography (EMG) electrodes, should be examined regularly for signs of irritation, infection, or device damage. EMG electrodes onto muscles should be closely monitored for signs of inflammation or infection. Unambiguous experimental endpoints should be established before any devices or hardware are implanted. These endpoints should indicate when devices or hardware should be removed because of failure, infection, or inflammation. Anticipating the potential consequences of implant failure before its occurrence is crucial for the viability of the study and animal well-being.

PROCEDURAL CONSIDERATIONS FOR ANESTHESIA, RESTRAINT, AND EUTHANASIA

ANESTHESIA AND ANALGESIA

Animal procedures are reviewed by the IACUC to ensure that proposed anesthetics and/or analgesics are appropriate for the species and research objectives. Written documentation of all surgical procedures, including the types, amounts, and time of administration of anesthetic, analgesic or tranquilizing drugs used and the physiologic parameters (i.e., heart rate, respiratory rate, body temperature, etc.) monitored during the procedure are required. This documentation is subject to inspection by the USDA veterinary inspectors and the IACUC. In addition, all manipulations and drug use should be recorded in the individual animal's record or the investigator's experimental notebook.

The ILAR guide for "the Care and Use of Laboratory Animals"[9] requires that any proposal to conduct painful procedures without anesthesia or analgesia be scientifically justified by the investigator and approved by the institutional animal care and use committee. Such procedures must be directly supervised by the responsible investigator.

Use of some anesthetic and analgesic agents are regulated by the Federal Drug Enforcement Administration (DEA).

Animals should be evaluated by performing a brief physical examination and recording baseline physiologic measurements of such parameters as body temperature, heart rate, and respiratory rate prior to the administration of an anesthetic agent. Animals should be weighed and dosages of agents administered calculated individually according to body weight measurements.

Suggested dosage for pre-anesthetics, tranquilizers, anesthetics, and analgesics are available online, and one resource is http://med.stanford.edu/compmed/animal_care/guidelines.html#anes.

Postsurgical care includes clinical observation of the animal to ensure uneventful recovery from anesthesia and surgery. Once the animal has been returned to its normal housing area, subsequent care may be necessary. This may include supportive fluids, analgesics, and other drugs as required; monitoring of the animal should include daily body temperatures, clinical observations for signs of pain, abnormal behavior, appetite and excretory functions, and providence of adequate care of surgical incisions. Written post-operative records including date, time, person making the observations, condition of animals, and any treatments/procedures performed should be maintained for inspection by USDA, IACUC, or other regulatory inspections.

MULTIPLE MAJOR SURGICAL PROCEDURES

Major surgery on the same animal may be needed for the sleep/behavioral monitoring. Major surgery penetrates and exposes a body cavity or produces substantial impairment of physical or physiologic function. Multiple major survival surgical procedures on a single animal are discouraged but may be permitted if scientifically justified by the user and approved by the IACUC. For example, multiple major survival surgical procedures can be justified if they are related components of a research project, or if they will conserve scarce animal resources. If multiple major survival surgery is approved, the IACUC should pay particular attention to animal well-being through continuing evaluation of outcomes. Cost savings alone is not an adequate reason for performing multiple major survival surgical procedures.

PAIN AND DISTRESS

It is critical to recognize and manage animal pain and distress. Although animals cannot communicate verbally, they exhibit motor behaviors and physiologic responses similar to those of humans in response to pain. These behaviors may include simple withdrawal reflexes, complex, unlearned behaviors such as vocalization and escape, and learned behaviors such as pressing a bar to avoid further exposure to noxious stimulation. When an animal is unable to completely adapt to a stressor and results in development of stress, an aversive state, it is defined as distress. The term distress encompasses the negative psychologic states that are sometimes associated with exposure to stressors, including fear, pain, malaise, anxiety, frustration, depression, and boredom. These states can manifest as maladaptive behaviors such as abnormal feeding or aggression or pathologic conditions that are not evident in behavior, such as hypertension and immunosuppression.[49]

Physical restraint is the use of manual or mechanical means to limit some or all of an animal's normal movement for the purpose of examination, collection of samples, drug administration, therapy, or experimental manipulation. Animals are restrained for brief periods, usually minutes, in most research applications. Animals can be physically restrained briefly either manually or with restraint devices. Restraint devices should be suitable in size, design, and operation to minimize discomfort or injury to the animal. Many dogs, nonhuman primates,[50] and other animals can be trained through use of positive reinforcement to present limbs or remain immobile for brief procedures. Prolonged restraint, including chairing of nonhuman primates, should be avoided unless it is essential for achieving research objectives and is approved by the IACUC. Less restrictive systems that do not limit an animal's ability to make normal postural adjustments, such as the tether system for nonhuman primates and stanchions for farm animals, should be used when compatible with protocol objectives.[51] When restraint devices are used, they should be specifically designed to accomplish research goals that are impossible or impractical to accomplish by other means or to prevent injury to animals or personnel. The following are important ILAR guidelines for restraint: (a) Restraint devices are not to be considered normal methods of housing. (b) Restraint devices should not be used simply as a convenience in handling or managing animals. (c) The period of restraint should be the minimum required to accomplish the research objectives. (d) Animals to be placed in restraint devices should be given training to adapt to the equipment and personnel. (e) Provision should be made for observation of the animal at appropriate intervals, as determined by the IACUC. (f) Veterinary care should be provided if lesions or illnesses associated with restraint are observed. The presence of lesions, illness, or severe behavioral change often necessitates temporary or permanent removal of the animal from restraint.

HEAD-RESTRAINT SYSTEMS

Head-restraint systems may also be used for sleep research using animals, such as in vivo electrophysiology. Head-restraint systems minimize the movement of the head during neurophysiology experiments without causing discomfort if the animal is properly conditioned.[48] A hardware, generically called a head-holder, is implanted chronically on the animal's skull. Small screws or bolts and dental acrylic or bone cement

Seiji Nishino, MD, PhD

anchor the head-holder to the skull. Then, during a training or experimental session, the head-holder is attached to a freestanding platform to immobilize the head. Besides minimizing movement, these systems provide a structural element for the anchor connectors from other surgically implanted monitoring devices, such as chronically implanted recording electrodes or indwelling cannulae/micodialys probes for delivery of pharmacological agents. They can also provide a superstructure through which microelectrodes are introduced into the brain for the recording of neural activity. Animals should be properly conditioned to restraint to eliminate any discomfort or stress that might be associated with it.

SLEEP DEPRIVATION

Sleep deprivation (SD) is a potentially useful strategy for studying the function of sleep, and thus is often applied to animal studies. Such short-term sleep loss does not appear to have marked adverse effects in humans or animals other than the progressive development of moderate to severe sleepiness, cognitive and performance impairment, and perhaps irritability or aggression.[52,53]

Short-term sleep loss in humans typically has no adverse physiologic consequences other than increasing sleepiness and impaired performance in some tasks.[52,53] In rats, biologically significant adverse effects (other than development of moderate to severe sleepiness and irritability or aggression) of sleep deprivation have been reported only after sleep deprivation of more than 5 days.[54,55] In a classic series of studies, Rechtschaffen and colleagues demonstrated that sleep deprivation in rats produces significant adverse effects only after SD of more than 5 days, but ultimately leads to death after 2-3 weels of sleep deprivation.[55] SD in this condition greatly increased body temperature and food intake, but weight fell rapidly. A stereotyped pattern of fur discoloration and skin lesions occurred. Finally, body temperature fell and death followed. No similar syndrome has been described in mice or other mammals commonly observed in laboratories, or in rats' sleep deprived by other means.

These authors used "disk-over-water" technique for SD; it can be used to deprive animals of REM sleep alone or both NREM and REM sleep.[56,57] The animals are housed on a rotating platform, or disk, that is positioned over a pan of water. When the electroencephalogram indicates that an animal is entering a state of sleep, a computer algorithm causes the disk to rotate at a low speed. The animal then generally awakens and walks to avoid contact with water. Another approach is forced locomotion, usually in a slowly revolving drum[58]. Interpretation of data collected with this method is confounded by the effect of continuous locomotion or exercise as opposed to the effects of sleep loss itself.[58]

There are several different methods to produce sleep deprivation in laboratory animals. The method most widely used is the so-called "gentle-handling" technique. This method has been applied to rodents, rabbits, and cats and is usually used to cause loss of both REM and NREM sleep. The animals are under continuous observation by the experimenter and are physically roused by the experimenter whenever they either enter a state of electroencephalographically defined sleep or assume a sleeplike posture. Animals are generally aroused by such actions as tapping on the cage, providing novel objects, or prodding gently, sometime with soft wire brushes. As the duration of the deprivation period increases, particularly beyond a few hours during the species' normal "rest" period, the experimenter must gradually increase the intensity or frequency of handling or of environmental stimulation to maintain arousal of the animal.

Another relatively common approach to inducing sleep loss in animals is the so-called "flowerpot" technique. This approach produces REM sleep deprivation by taking advantage of the muscle atony that develops during REM sleep.[59] The animals (typically rats) are placed on a small platform (historically an inverted flowerpot) in a tank of water. The platform is large enough to allow the rat to engage in slow-wave sleep, in which residual muscle tone allows it to retain a stable sleeping posture. However, as the animal enters REM sleep and develops skeletal-muscle atonia, it slips from the platform into the water and awakens.

The flowerpot method of REM sleep deprivation causes alterations in several biochemical indexes of stress.[60] In a refined form of the flowerpot and disk-over-water methods, multiple platforms are used in one large pool so that animals can engage in locomotor activity.[60] This technique is also used only for REM sleep deprivation.

In contrast with the gentle-handling method, the flowerpot and disk-over-water techniques can be easily imposed for long periods, and these approaches create some animal-use concerns. The duration of sleep deprivation must be well justified scientifically, particularly if it will be continuous for more than a few days. Animals that are maintained on chronic sleep-deprivation schedules should be closely monitored for injury and general well-being, and observations should be recorded. The task is simplified by the fact that research teams typically monitor such animals very closely to ensure that they are experiencing the targeted amount of sleep loss.

GUIDELINES FOR ENDPOINT MONITORING AND HUMANE TERMINATION

Endpoints are established for both experimental and humane reasons. An experimental endpoint is chosen to mark the planned end of an experimental manipulation and associated data gathering. In order to comply with guidelines governing the use of animals in experimentation, the use of death as an endpoint to experimental manipulation, rather than performing euthanasia to humanely terminate an animal, is discouraged. Directors must perform euthanasia on all moribund experimental animals unless there is scientific justification that euthanasia would invalidate experimental data collection.

Moribund is defined as "in a dying state." Animals are considered to be moribund if they manifest any of the following clinical signs: Inability to ambulate that prevents the animal's easy access to food and/or water. Inability to maintain itself in an upright position. Prolonged (greater than 48 hours) inappetence and/or clinical dehydration. Agonal breathing and cyanosis; chronic diarrhea or constipation. Hematologic or biochemical parameters that indicate organ failure incompatible with life. Unconsciousness with no response to external stimuli such as a toe-pinch withdrawal test. If killing a moribund animal would invalidate the study, the scientific justification for using death as an endpoint must be provided in writing as part of the animal care protocol and must be approved by the IACUC prior to initiating this procedure.

EUTHANASIA

Euthanasia is generally performed at the end of a project or, if possible, during a procedure in which animals experience severe or chronic pain or distress that cannot be relieved.[47] Since there may be a need to euthanize animals for unanticipated reasons even on protocols that do not include euthanasia as part of the planned project, at least one method must be documented for each species used in a protocol. The euthanasia method chosen must be appropriate for the species and research use described by the protocol and must be consistent with the recommendations of the American Veterinary Medical Association Panel on Euthanasia.[61] If the method deviates from AVMA recommendations, the deviation must be justified scientifically and approved by the IACUC. Euthanasia should be performed quickly and efficiently in a nonpublic area and generally not in rooms in which animals are housed.

Laboratory animals can be euthanized in three ways: Hypoxia, depression of neural activity necessary for life function, and physical disruption of brain activity and destruction of neurons necessary for life.[62]

However, the physiology of the perinatal animal renders some of the euthanasia methods used for adult animals inadequate and therefore inadvisable.[9] In rodent fetuses that are less than E14, the lack of neural development prevents signs of fetal response to noxious stimuli, so euthanasia of the dam or removal of the fetus from the dam will result in the painless death of the fetus without a requirement for additional measures.[63] Inhalant agents, including inhalant anesthetics and CO_2, that cause death by cerebral depression and/or hypoxia, must be used carefully for euthanasia of older fetuses or neonates. The comparatively hypoxic intrauterine environment renders these young animals much more tolerant of hypoxic conditions than adults, and euthanasia with an agent that causes death by hypoxia, such as CO_2, may take 30 minutes or longer. Therefore, if these agents are used, personnel should be appropriately trained to use prolonged exposure times. Ideally, death should be verified by a secondary method such as decapitation or cervical dislocation. Older fetuses and neonates can also be euthanized with chemical anesthetics, decapitation, or cervical dislocation. If chemical fixation of the whole fetus is necessary, the fetus should be properly anesthetized before fixation.[63] In accordance with the report of the AVMA Panel on Euthanasia,[61] some physical methods of euthanasia, such as decapitation, require appropriate training, experience, and specific approval by the IACUC.

REFERENCES

1. Nishino S, Fujiki N. Animal models of sleep disorders. In: Tatlisumak T, Fisher M, eds. Handbook of Experimental Neurology. Cambridge: Cambridge University Press; 2006:504-43.

2. ICSD-2, ed. ICSD-2-International classification of sleep disorders, 2nd ed.: Diagnostic and coding manual. Westchester, Illinois: American Academy of Sleep Medicine 2005. Medicine AAoS, ed.

3. Lin L, Faraco J, Li R, et al. The sleep disorder canine narcolepsy is caused by a mutation in the hypocretin (orexin) receptor 2 gene. Cell 1999;98:365-76.

4. Chemelli RM, Willie JT, Sinton CM, et al. Narcolepsy in orexin knockout mice: molecular genetics of sleep regulation. Cell 1999;98:437-51.

5. Peyron C, Faraco J, Rogers W, et al. A mutation in a case of early onset narcolepsy and a generalized absence of hypocretin peptides in human narcoleptic brains. Nat Med 2000;6:991-7.

6. Nishino S, Ripley B, Overeem S, Lammers GJ, Mignot E. Hypocretin (orexin) deficiency in human narcolepsy. Lancet 2000;355:39-40.

7. Fujiki N, Nishino S. Hypocretin/orexin replacement therapy in hypocretin/orexin deficient narcolepsy: an overview. In: Nishino S, Sakurai T, eds. The Orexin/Hypocretin System:Physiology and Pathophysiology. Totowa: Humana Press; 2006:367-88.

8. Checklist for Review of Vertebrate Animal Section (VAS). http://grants.nih.gov/grants/olaw/VASchecklist.pdf.

9. Council IoLARCoLSNR. Guide for the Care and Use of Laboratory Animals. Washington, D.C.: National Academy Press; 1996.

10. Research IoLARCoGftUoAiNaB. Guidelines for the Use of Animals in Neuroscience and Behavioral Research. Washington, D.C.: National Academy Press.

11. Zepelin H, Siegel JM, Tobler I. Mammalian sleep. In: Kryger MH, Roth T, Dement WC, eds. Principles and Practice of Sleep Medicine. 4th ed. Philadelphia: Elsevier Saunders; 2005:91-100.

12. Tobler I. Phylogeny of sleep reguration. In: Kryger MH, Roth T, Dement WC, eds. Principles and Practice of Sleep Medicine. 4th ed. Philadelphia: Elsevier Saunders; 2005:77-90.

13. Revel FG, Gottowik J, Gatti S, Wettstein JG, Moreau JL. Rodent models of insomnia: a review of experimental procedures that induce sleep disturbances. Neurosci Biobehav Rev 2009;33:874-99.

14. Vitaterna MH, King DP, Chang AM, et al. Mutagenesis and mapping of a mouse gene clock, essential for circadian behavior. Science 1994;264:719-25.

15. King DP, Takahashi JS. Molecular genetics of circadian rhythms in mammals. Annu Rev Neurosci 2000; 23:713-42.

16. Reppert SM, Weaver DR. Molecular analysis of mammalian circadian rhythms. Annu Rev Physiol 2001; 63:647-76.

17. Berrettini WH, Ferraro TN, Alexander RC, Buchberg AM, Vogel WH. Quantitative trait loci mapping of three loci controlling morphine preference using inbred mouse strains. Nat Genet 1994;7:54-8.

18. Franken P, Chollet D, Tafti M. The homeostatic regulation of sleep need is under genetic control. J Neurosci 2001;21:2610-21.

19. Tafti M, Chollet D, Valatx JL, Franken P. Quantitative trait loci approach to the genetics of sleep in recombinant inbred mice. J Sleep Res 1999;8 Suppl 1:37-43.

20. Borbély AA. Sleep Homeostatsis and Models of Sleep Regulation. Second ed. Philadelphia: W.B. Saunders Company; 1994.

21. Mackiewicz M, Paigen B, Naidoo N, Pack AI. Analysis of the QTL for sleep homeostasis in mice: Homer1a is a likely candidate. Physiol Genomics 2008;33:91-9.

22. Maret S, Dorsaz S, Gurcel L, et al. Homer1a is a core brain molecular correlate of sleep loss. Proc Natl Acad Sci USA 2007;104:20090-5.

23. Capecchi MR. The new mouse genetics: altering the genome by gene targeting. Trends Genet Mar 1989;5:70-6.

24. Jaenisch R. Transgenic animals. Science 1988;240:1468-74.

25. Williams RS, Wagner PD. Transgenic animals in integrative biology: approaches and interpretations of outcome. J Appl Physiol 2000;88:1119-26.

26. Beuckmann CT, Sinton CM, Williams SC, et al. Expression of a poly-glutamine-ataxin-3 transgene in orexin neurons induces narcolepsy-cataplexy in the rat. J Neurosci 2004;24:4469-77.

27. Hara J, Beuckmann CT, Nambu T, et al. Genetic ablation of orexin neurons in mice results in narcolepsy, hypophagia, and obesity. Neuron 2001;30:345-54.

28. Twigger S, Lu J, Shimoyama M, et al. Rat Genome Database (RGD): mapping disease onto the genome. Nucleic Acids Res 2002;30:125-8.

29. Ueda S, Kawamata M, Teratani T, et al. Establishment of rat embryonic stem cells and making of chimera rats. PLoS One 2008;3:e2800.

30. Bucan M, Abel T. The mouse: genetics meets behaviour. Nat Rev Genet 2002;3:114-23.

31. Lewandoski M. Conditional control of gene expression in the mouse. Nat Rev Genet 2001;2:743-55.

32. Akagi K, Sandig V, Vooijs M, et al. Cre-mediated somatic site-specific recombination in mice. Nucleic Acids Res 1997;25:1766-73.

33. Weiss B, Davidkova G, Zhang SP. Antisense strategies in neurobiology. Neurochem Int 1997;31:321-48.

34. Cirelli C, Pompeiano M, Arrighi P, Tononi G. Sleep-waking changes after c-fos antisense injections in the medial preoptic area. Neuroreport 1995;6:801-5.

35. Xi MC, Morales FR, Chase MH. Evidence that wakefulness and REM sleep are controlled by a GABAergic pontine mechanism. J Neurophysiol 1999;82:2015-9.

36. Thakkar MM, Ramesh V, Strecker RE, McCarley RW. Microdialysis perfusion of orexin-A in the basal forebrain increases wakefulness in freely behaving rats. Arch Ital Biol 2001;139:313-28.

37. Hammond SM, Bernstein E, Beach D, Hannon GJ. An RNA-directed nuclease mediates post-transcriptional gene silencing in Drosophila cells. Nature 2000;404:293-6.

38. Hendricks JC, Sehgal A, Pack AI. The need for a simple animal model to understand sleep. Prog Neurobiol 2000;61:339-51.

39. Campbell SS, Tobler I. Animal sleep: a review of sleep duration across phylogeny. Neurosci Biobehav Rev 1984;8:269-300.

40. Desarnaud F, Murillo-Rodriguez E, Lin L, et al. The Diurnal Rhythm of Hypocretin in Young and Old F344 Rats. Sleep 2004;27:851-6.

Seiji Nishino, MD, PhD

41. Bakehe M, Miramand JL, Chambille B, Gaultier C, Escourrou P. Cardiovascular changes during acute episodic repetitive hypoxic and hypercapnic breathing in rats. Eur Respir J 1995;8:1675-80.

42. Fletcher EC, Bao G. Effect of episodic eucapnic and hypocapnic hypoxia on systemic blood pressure in hypertension-prone rats. J Appl Physiol 1996;81:2088-94.

43. Bao G, Metreveli N, Fletcher EC. Acute and chronic blood pressure response to recurrent acoustic arousal in rats. Am J Hypertens 1999;12:504-10.

44. Committee) IIRA. US Government Principles for the Utiliza tion and Care of Vertebrate Animals Used in Testing, Research, and Training. Washington, D.C: IRAC (Interagency Research Animal Committee); 1985.

45. Dell RB, Holleran S, Ramakrishnan R. Sample size determination. Ilar J 2002;43:207-213.

46. Regulations) CCoF. Title 9 (Animals and Animal Products). Subchapter A (Animal Welfare). Washington, D.C.: Office of the Federal Register; 1985.

47. Service) PPH. Public Health Service Policy on Humane Care and Use of Laboratory Animals. Washington, D.C.: U.S. Department of Health and Human Services; 1996.

48. NIH. Methods and Welfare Considerations in Behavioral Research with Animals. Washington, DC: U.S. Government Printing Office; 2002.

49. NRC. Recognition and Alleviation of Pain and Distress in Laboratory Animals. Washington, DC: National Academy Press; 1992.

50. Reinhardt V. Restraint methods of laboratory nonhuman primates: a critical review. Anim. Welf 1995;4:221-38.

51. Morton WR, Knitter GH, Smith PM, Susor TG, Schmitt K. Alternatives to chronic restraint of nonhuman primates. J Am Vet Med Assoc 1987;191:1282-86.

52. Horne JA, Pettitt AN. High incentive effects on vigilance performance during 72 hours of total sleep deprivation. Acta Psychol (Amst) 1985;58:123-39.

53. Naitoh P, Kelly TL, Englund C. Health effects of sleep deprivation. Occup Med 1990;5:209-237.

54. Everson CA, Toth LA. Systemic bacterial invasion induced by sleep deprivation. Am J Physiol Regul Integr Comp Physiol 2000;278:R905-16.

55. Rechtschaffen A, Bergmann BM. Sleep deprivation in the rat: an update of the 1989 paper. Sleep 2002;25:18-24.

56. Bergmann BM, Kushida CA, Everson CA, Gilliland MA, Obermeyer W, Rechtschaffen A. Sleep deprivation in the rat: II. Methodology. Sleep 1989;12:5-12.

57. Rechtschaffen A, Gilliland MA, Bergmann BM, Winter JB. Physiological correlates of prolonged sleep deprivation in rats. Science 1983;221:182-4.

58. Rechtschaffen A, Bergmann BM, Gilliland MA, Bauer K. Effects of method, duration, and sleep stage on rebounds from sleep deprivation in the rat. Sleep 1999;22:11–31.

59. Cohen HB, Dement WC. Sleep: Changes in threshold to electroconvulsive shock in rats after deprivation of "paradoxical" phase. Science 1965;150:1318–9.

60. Suchecki D, Tiba PA, Tufik S. Paradoxical sleep deprivation facilitates subsequent corticosterone response to a mild stressor in rats. Neurosci Lett 2002;320:45-8.

61. AVMA Guidelines on Euthanasia (Formerly Report of the AVMA Panel on Euthanasia). http://www.avma.org/issues/animal_welfare/euthanasia.pdf

62. Balaban RS, Hampshire VA. Challenges in small animal noninvasive imaging. ILAR J 2001;42:248-62.

63. NIH. Intramural Guidelines for the Euthanasia of Mouse and Rat Fetuses and Neonates. 1997:Available from: http://www.nal.usda.gov/awic/legislat/neonate.htm

64. Nishino S, Honda K, Reid M, Dement WC, Mignot E. Acetylcholine release and neuronal activity in the basal forebrain of freely-moving narcoleptic Dobermans. Sleep Res 1997;26:444.

65. Cano G, Mochizuki T, Saper CB. Neural circuitry of stress-induced insomnia in rats. J Neurosci 2008;28:10167-84.

66. Lu J, Greco MA, Shiromani P, Saper CB. Effect of lesions of the ventrolateral preoptic nucleus on NREM and REM sleep. J Neurosci 2000;20:3830-42.

67. Hendricks JC, Kline LR, Kovalski RJ, O'Brien JA, Morrison AR, Pack AI. The English bulldog: a natural model of sleep-disordered breathing. J Appl Physiol 1987;63:1344-50.

68. Yasuma F, Kozar LF, Kimoff RJ, Bradley TD, Phillipson EA. Interaction of chemical and mechanical respiratory stimuli in the arousal response to hypoxia in sleeping dogs. Am Rev Respir Dis 1991;143:1274-7.

69. Carley DW, Trbovic S, Radulovacki M. Sleep apnea in normal and REM sleep-deprived normotensive Wistar-Kyoto and spontaneously hypertensive (SHR) rats. Physiol Behav 1996;59:827-31.

70. Nakamura A, Kuwaki T. Sleep apnea in mice: a useful animal model for study of SIDS? Early Hum Dev 2003;75 Suppl:S167-74.

71. Hendricks JC, Lager A, O'Brien D, Morrison AR. Movement disorders during sleep in cats and dogs. J Am Vet Med Assoc 1989;194:686-9.

72. Okura M, Fujiki N, Ripley B, et al. Narcoleptic canines display periodic leg movements during sleep. Psychiatry Clin Neurosci 2001;55:243-4.

73. Baier PC, Winkelmann J, Hohne A, Lancel M, Trenkwalder C. Assessment of spontaneously occurring periodic limb movements in sleep in the rat. J Neurol Sci 2002;198:71-7.

74. Ondo WG, Zhao HR, Le WD. Animal models of restless legs syndrome. Sleep Med 2007;8:344-8.

75. Hendricks JC. Invited review: Sleeping flies don't lie: the use of Drosophila melanogaster to study sleep and circadian rhythms. J Appl Physiol 2003;94:1660-72; discussion 1673.

76. Cirelli C. Searching for sleep mutants of Drosophila melanogaster. Bioessays 2003;25:940-949.

77. Yokogawa T, Zhang J, Renier C, Mignot E. Characterization of a sleep-like state in adult zebrafish. Sleep 2004;27(Abstract Supplement):A84.

78. Renier CM, Rosa FM, Mignot E. Pharmacogenomics of sleep-promoting drugs in zebrafish. Sleep 2004;27(Abstract Supplement):A389.

Seiji Nishino, MD, PhD

CHAPTER VII

WRITING THE GRANT PROPOSAL

Clifford B. Saper, MD, PhD

GENERAL TIPS FOR SUCCESSFUL GRANT WRITING

The most important step before sitting down to write the grant proposal is to frame the question that you will be investigating. This requires discussion with colleagues, mentors, and most especially Program staff. The National Institutes of Health (NIH), and also many other funders, have staff members who manage grants in a particular area or field. At the NIH, these individuals are called Program Directors. Once you know the area in which you are planning to write, it is a good idea to contact Program Directors from Institutes that address the area in which you plan to work. The Program Director can help you frame the proposal in a way that will be fundable. They sometimes will read the proposal and give you advice. Once they are interested in a proposal, they will attend the study section meeting and often can give you general feedback if you need to resubmit. Or, the Program Director can decide to "special" fund a grant, taking one that is beyond the automatic payline, and selecting it for funding because it is important to the portfolio of research that the Program Directors manages.

The Program Director can also help you choose a study section (or Initial Review Group, IRG). They know the personalities of the different study sections, and which are likely to have the right balance of expertise and interest in your area. You should also review the IRGs in the NIH Web site, and see which ones have appropriate expertise to review your proposal. The exact list of reviewers for your grant will not be the same as is on the Web site, because some study sections members will not be there, some new ones will be added, and most study sections use additional *ad hoc* reviewers who review only a few grants in a cycle, and do not vote on them. But the list will give you an idea of which study section to target your proposal for. Once you and the Program Director have agreed on this, it is important that you write a cover letter for your proposal, indicating that you have discussed this with the Program Director, who has suggested that study section. The Center for Scientific Review (CSR) at the NIH is independent, and can assign your proposal differently. It often will take that advice if it comes from a Program Director, but frequently does not honor the request if it comes from the investigator alone. The rest of the grant should also be structured to insure that it is assigned to the Program and study section that is requested (see Abstract and Specific Aims, pg 86).

Once the overall question that is being investigated has been selected, the next step is to break this down into smaller Specific Aims that can each be addressed by a set of experiments. It is important that the overall question be important, but also that it can be approached by means of a series of sharply defined experiments, which will produce clear answers, and that these answers will test the overall hypothesis in critical ways.

Many investigators do not understand the concept of a hypothesis vs. a test of the hypothesis. A hypothesis is literally a theory about how something works. You can then draw out from that hypothesis a variety of critical tests that can potentially falsify the hypothesis. A test never "proves" a hypothesis. But if a series of tests fail to falsify the hypothesis, the hypothesis is strengthened. Those tests constitute the Specific Aims of the proposal. You are looking for a hypothesis that is sufficiently interesting and exciting that it is worth investigating, and which can produce a series of concrete and sharp tests.

The second major principle of grant writing is to remember the audience you are writing for. In general, the person reading your proposal is likely to be a scientist in a related field, but not directly in your field. This person will not know all of the literature in your field, and it will pay for you to give a straightforward and thorough review of the literature that is critical for your work. The reviewer is typically a midcareer scientist, who will be reading your grant over several evenings, while the television is playing in the background, the kids are fighting, and the dog needs to be taken out for a walk. There will be interruptions, and it may take several days to get through your proposal, then several days to get around to writing the critique. You should therefore plan to be deliberately redundant in providing information. As you will see from the following sections, you should plan to build into each section of the proposal a review of what you have already established and a preview of what is coming next. You should try to "think like the reviewer" in identifying potential weaknesses that might be identified, and then either correcting them, or including a discussion of them in the Problems and Pitfalls section (see Experimental Design, pg 89). Make life as easy as possible for the reviewer, and the reviewer will pay you back with a much better score.

A third general principle is that you should avoid abbreviations. Many proposals include so many abbreviations that by the third or fourth page, it looks like they are being written in code. Define the abbreviations in each section (not just once at the beginning, where they may be hard to find) or in a small table, and try to use no more than half a dozen for the entire proposal. Similarly, avoid lab jargon. You may have a cute name for a paradigm or a preparation in the lab, but you should leave it there, and describe things with clear English.

SECTIONS OF THE GRANT PROPOSAL

ABSTRACT

The abstract is the first part of the grant that the reviewer will see, but for that reason is the part that you should write last. A well-structured abstract helps the reviewer get a sense of what is to come, including the question you are asking, the specific aims, and the methods you are using. It should include a brief indication of the importance of the work as well. In general, this structure is not greatly different from the abstract in a paper, except you cannot describe the outcome, only the studies to be done. Because it is necessary to know how the entire proposal lays out before you write the abstract, it is generally a good practice to do this after the body of the proposal is in place.

The abstract is also the first part of the grant that is encountered by the Center for Scientific Review, and so plays an important role in assigning the proposal to a specific Program and study section. In general, the CSR staff are looking for words that identify a particular institute. For example, a proposal on mechanisms of cognitive impairment with sleep loss can be written to emphasize the cognitive issues (in which case it is likely to be assigned to the National Institute of Mental Health [NIMH] or National Institute of Neurologic Disorders and Stroke [NINDS], depending upon which cognitive deficits are being studied); it can be written to emphasize the sleep loss itself as an issue, in which case it is likely to be assigned to National Heart, Lung, and Blood Institute (NHLBI); or it can be written to emphasize a disease process that causes the sleep loss (with narcolepsy leading the grant to an NINDS assignment; insomnia to an NIMH assignment; aging to an National Institute on Aging [NIA] assignment; or sleep apnea to an NHLBI assignment). You should target your proposal to the Program Director you have worked with by emphasizing in the abstract (and the first paragraph of the Specific Aims) the issues specific to that institute. Similarly, the study sections generally have expertise in specific areas. If you want to target your proposal to a specific study section, you should mention issues related to the expertise of that study section early in your Abstract and Specific Aims.

SPECIFIC AIMS

In many ways, the Specific Aims are the most important part of your proposal. Although they should be relatively brief (no more than two pages in the current 20 page NIH proposal; this could be shorter in the future, or in proposals to other organizations that permit fewer pages), they put in place the rationale and the methods, and they must capture the imagination of the reviewer, or you will not be funded. Most proposals that are triaged (lower 50%) without discussion are ones where the Specific Aims were judged by the reviewers to be insufficiently exciting to merit a full discussion. It is possible to overcome technical objections to your proposal, but lack of excitement is a fatal flaw in all cases.

You should plan to start with a brief (one or two paragraphs) summary of the overall problem and your hypothesis (or hypotheses). It is very important to give a summary of the background for your proposal (which you will develop in detail in the next section) in a succinct and readable way here, so that a non-specialist in your area will be able to understand the importance and excitement in what you plan to do. You would like your background discussion to end with a clear hypothesis or theory that explains some important observations in your field. This should be highlighted. When possible, it is nice to include a summary diagram or cartoon that outlines your hypothesis for the reader.

This introduction should be followed by brief descriptions of the Specific Aims. It is best to have separate paragraphs for each aim, beginning with the Specific Aim number, and a brief (one sentence) aim, which should be printed in bold. It often helps to frame the Specific Aims as questions, but they can be framed narratively. For example, if you are studying the effects of sleep apnea on cognitive function, you might hypothesize that the depth of the intermittent hypoxias might correlate with neuronal injury and long term cognitive deficits. To test this hypothesis, your first aim might be to correlate the degree of hypoxia during apneas with function on cognitive testing. You could frame this as:

Specific Aim 1: To determine the effects of degree of hypoxia during sleep apnea on cognitive function.

Or you might state the same aim:

Specific Aim 1: What is the effect of degree of hypoxia during sleep apnea on cognitive function?

The point of this aim is to provide a critical test of the hypothesis, as if the degree of hypoxia does not correlate with the deficit, the hypothesis will be falsified.

You should next describe the aim in a brief paragraph. This should include a sentence or two each on the rationale, the methods to be employed, and what you think the aim might show. For example, for the Aim above, this might be:

Specific Aim 1: To determine the effects of degree of hypoxia during sleep apnea on cognitive function.

Patients with obstructive sleep apnea (OSA) are subjected to repeated cycles of hypoxia during sleep. While prolonged hypoxia is known to damage neurons in cortical and hippocampal areas necessary for cognitive function, the effects of brief, repeated hypoxia on the function of these systems is not known. We will use neuropsychological measures of memory, executive function, and sensory and motor processing time to determine if there is a correlation between the amount of hypoxia during sleep in patients with OSA and cognitive performance.

Note that the abbreviation for OSA is explained the first time it is used.

BACKGROUND AND SIGNIFICANCE

The first two paragraphs of the Specific Aims section should have already summarized the substance of your background and significance section. However, this is your opportunity to lay out the concepts clearly and succinctly, and discuss them critically. The purpose is both to bring a reader from another field up to speed, and to impress a reader within your field with your scholarly approach to the accumulated evidence.

Hence, it is important that this section is fair and balanced, striking a tone similar to a review article. If you take an advocacy stance, and cite evidence only that favors your ideas, while ignoring evidence to the contrary, you will undermine your credibility. Also, remember that the person reading the proposal may well be one of the individuals who has worked in the field. Thus, it is worthwhile to scan the list of study section members, and make sure their work is covered. However, because you cannot predict who else might be invited as an *ad hoc* reviewer, you should cast a broad net in respecting the opinions and work of other scientists in the field.

The Background and Significance should be broken down into a series of subsections, each of which should have a title phrase. For example, in the example used for the Specific Aim 1, the subject headings might be:

Evidence for the effect of brief, repetitive hypoxia on nerve cell function in vitro.

Evidence for the effect of brief, repetitive hypoxemia on cortical and hippocampal neurons in vivo.

Effects of brief, repetitive hypoxemia on cognitive function in animals and humans.

Your goal is to have at least one paragraph addressing the work to be done in each Specific Aim, in which you make clear the limits of what is known, and why it is important to find the information that the Specific Aim will supply. You should plan to end that paragraph with a statement along the lines of: "For this reason, in Specific Aim 1, we will test for those things that are not yet known."

One or two well chosen figures in the Background and Significance section can greatly increase its impact. Look for summary diagrams that illustrate principles in previous work, or key graphs or other illustrations that clarify important points.

PRELIMINARY DATA/PROGRESS REPORT

This section of the proposal has three very different aims: First, you want to use it to provide additional data from your own experiments that will make the need for the experiments in the Specific Aims even clearer and more acute. One problem faced by many new grant writers is the line dividing up your own work between the Background and Significance and the Preliminary Data. You should already have cited the data from your own published work in the previous section. It is permissible in that section to foreshadow your unpublished work (e.g., "As we will show in the Preliminary Data, we have now provided additional evidence that there is slowing of cortical processing time for sensory responses in patients with OSA.") However, you should save the actual presentation of those experiments and result for the Preliminary Data section. Similarly, you should plan to provide a brief summary of your previous published work in leading up to the rationale for your new Preliminary Data, but should not repeat that information in any detail (e.g., "As we showed in the Background and Significance, our earlier work demonstrated a slowing in motor response time in patients with OSA. We therefore tested sensory processing times as well."). Remember that the reader may be reading the two sections back to back, and be annoyed by unnecessary repetition. But he or she may be reading the sections days apart, and so a brief reminder of the previous section is always useful.

The second aim of the Preliminary Results section is to demonstrate that you can do the experiments that you plan to do. This is particularly necessary if your new experiments require a method you have not previously used in your published work. In that case, some examples showing that you have mastered the method in a context other than the project you propose can be useful in convincing the reader of your ability to carry out the project as planned. In the example above, if you have never done a sensory processing task, you might want to have a section showing that you have successfully used this task (perhaps in a different project, as yet unpublished), and provide some examples of the data.

The third aim is to provide some actual Preliminary Results to whet the appetite of your reader. This always involves walking a tightrope, because if you display enough results to give a solid answer, then there is no longer any reason to do the project. But if you only show the results from one subject, the reader may think that this is simply random variation. For this reason, most investigators tend to give preliminary results from a small cohort which does not have the statistical power to answer the primary question, but does have responses "in the right direction" to support the hypothesis.

Clearly there are many other approaches to providing Preliminary Results (e.g., providing results of collateral studies that are different from, but support the main goal of the ones you propose). However, the same principles apply to how you describe the Preliminary Results.

The Preliminary Results should be divided (like the Background and Significance) into sections, each of which should be introduced by a brief title. Each section should have a distinct purpose that should be clear to the reader (i.e., it should validate your ability to perform the studies in a Specific Aim; it should support why it is necessary to do a Specific Aim; or it should show preliminary results from doing a Specific Aim). You should end the section with a statement of what that preliminary result provides, such as "These results demonstrate that we can measure small differences in sensory processing times in a robust and reproducible fashion, which will be necessary for Specific Aim 1."

It is a good idea to use graphics wherever possible in the Preliminary Results. In many proposals, each section is supported by a figure of some sort, representing the results. This not only reduces the amount of text that it takes to provide your results (a good picture is worth a thousand words...), but it also reinforces the quality of your findings.

Note that for competing renewal proposals, this section also must contain a Progress Report. We have not dwelled on this, because this manual is meant for new investigators. However, at some point a new investigator hopes to become one competing for renewal, so some mention is worthwhile. The Progress Report is a two-edged sword. For a project that has produced important publications and which the investigator plans to continue in a similar vein, it is an opportunity to shine. The published papers become part of the Background and Significance and can be briefly reprised, while the unpublished studies become part of the Preliminary Data. There is minimal duplication and the clear progress that has been made provides a strong boost to the investigator. On the other hand, if the project has not made strong progress in its previous cycle, or if the investigator wants to change directions, the Progress Report becomes a millstone around his or her neck. Lack of progress undermines the future plans. And if the investigator has to include a lot of work from the previous cycle that is not relevant to the new project, valuable space is lost in which new work could have been described. For this reason, experienced investigators may decide to submit a new grant, rather than a renewal, even for a successful project, based on a strategic decision about the value of the Progress Report.

EXPERIMENTAL DESIGN

The Experimental Design is the heart of the proposal. It typically occupies half or more of the total proposal, and it requires exquisitely detailed attention. It is here where you will either make your case for your work and satisfy the reviewer that you have the ability to do the work, or not.

The Experimental Design may begin with a brief introductory paragraph, but the body of it should be divided into two segments. The first should address the design of each Specific Aim. The second should provide General Methods that are too bulky to include within the Aim.

The structure of the description of the Experimental Design for each Specific Aim should begin with a

Clifford B. Saper, MD, PhD

restatement of that Aim, exactly as it appeared in the first section. This should then be followed by a series of paragraphs that provide necessary information about that Aim. Each paragraph should be headed by the title describing it, as in this example:

Specific Aim 1: To determine the effects of degree of hypoxia during sleep apnea on cognitive function.

  Rationale.

  Experimental design.

  Data analysis.

  Anticipated outcomes and interpretions.

  Potential problems and pitfalls.

Note that the information in these paragraphs parallels the brief description of the aim that was presented in the first section. This is deliberate, and it allows the reviewer to go back at a later time and get a gestalt of the entire project from the initial two page description, or to dive into the details of the individual Specific Aims as needed. Repetition of information, for the harried reviewer who may read your work over several sittings is essential, as long as it does not take up too much space.

The **Rationale** is a brief repetition of why you want to do this Specific Aim. It should be only a few sentences long, and should briefly summarize your reasoning, provided in the Background and Significance and Preliminary Results. The reader can be referred back to those sections for any lengthy discussions, but it is important that the reason for doing the experiments is clear.

The **Experimental Design** should be just that, a design, not a detailed, blow-by-blow description of how you actually do the experiments. It should contain enough detail that the reviewer knows essentially what you are doing, but you should put the details of the actual experiments into the General Methods section, and note that in the text of the Experimental Design. It is important that this section gives the overall information about the groups of subjects, number in each group, and how they relate to each other (e.g., which treatments they will receive, or which measures will be made). This section should be one or two paragraphs long, and should provide an overview of the study, so that a reader can follow how the data will be analyzed.

The **Data Analysis** section is in many ways the most important, as it describes how you are going to draw important information out of your results. Surprisingly, this section is often omitted entirely in proposals from novices, who tend to feel that it should be intuitive what you will do with your results. This is not the case.

In the example above, you may have data from sleep studies that indicates the periods of hypoxemia and how profound they were, as well as data from several cognitive tests. For the hypoxemia, you have to choose a measure that will indicate the degree of hypoxemia that was experienced. You could use the number of periods (but this does not tell you if they were very profound), the depth of the worst hypoxemia (or perhaps the mean of the depth of the 5 or 10 or 20 worst events), or perhaps the total "area under the curve" for time vs. oxygen level below a certain threshold. You need to decide which of these measures more accurately reflects what you are trying to measure, and to explain how it will be done. For the cognitive testing, each test may return multiple measures (e.g., reaction time, accuracy, etc.) You need to explain which measures you will use. Finally, you have to describe how you will explore the relationships of the two types of data. Will you divide the subjects into two groups (mild vs. profound hypoxemia) based on some threshold criterion, and compare their test results as groups? Will you do a regression or multivariate analysis?

Before writing this section, if you are not experienced with statistics, it is important to review your plans with someone who is. You should also plan to do a power analysis, based on your preliminary data, to show that it is likely that you will be able to obtain a statistically valid answer with the group sizes you plan.

The **Anticipated Results and Interpretations** also are often overlooked by novice grant writers, who feel that the meaning of their results should be obvious. However, to a reader from another field, the connections with the earlier data in the field have to be made explicitly. Thus, in our example, you might write: "Based upon our Preliminary Results, we expect to find a range of hypoxemia, as measured by area under the curve with a 95 percent threshold. We expect that the group defined as "severe hypoxemia," the upper 25 percent of this group, will have statistically significant increases in sensory reaction times, increased inaccuracy in response, and poorer scores in short term memory testing, the Wisconsin card sorting task, and the Sternberg test of dorsolateral prefrontal function. We also expect that there will be a statistically significant correlation on regression testing of each of these measures with degree of hypoxemia. We will interpret these results as indicating that the subjects with the worst hypoxemia have had damage to cortical and hippocampal circuitry necessary to sustain these complex cognitive responses."

Note that it is important not just to explain how you expect the tests to come out, but also what that means for your overall hypothesis. This section, in effect, closes the loop between the introduction and the actual study results.

The **Potential Problems and Pitfalls** section has two purposes. First, it allows you to consider the potential confounds to your results, and how you will deal with them. It also gives you the ability to anticipate how you will handle a failure to find what you want.

The critical reviewer will be looking for potential confounds in your work, and almost certainly will find a few. Your job in this section is to anticipate what the reviewer may find, and to provide a response that you otherwise might have to provide in the Introduction to your revised application, after this one is rejected for funding. It is important to ask colleagues for help here, and to set your proposal aside for a few days, and approach it like a reviewer who was determined to find ways to prevent your proposal from being funded. If you do your job well here, the reviewer will be relieved to find that you have considered the problems he or she has turned up, and that you already have reasonable answers to them.

In our example, you may realize that the patients with the worst hypoxia also have the worst hypercarbia. You could explain that hypercarbia is not associated with neuronal injury. You could provide evidence from studies in patients with hypoxemia without hypercarbia that there is comparable cognitive impairment after the hypoxia is corrected. Or you could offer to do an additional study at a later time, after the patients have been on continuous positive airway pressure (CPAP), to retest them, if your results of the present study turn out the way you want them to. Note that the ability to propose later projects is a two edged sword. The reviewer may wonder why you did not include this as a separate aim in the current proposal. However, if the need for additional studies is dependent upon a certain outcome that will not be clear until late in the project, then you have a good rationale for not including it in the current application. The point here, though, is that you have wide-ranging ability to suggest a variety of reasonable responses to potential criticisms, and this can defuse possible criticisms of your work by the referee.

The second issue to deal with is how the failure of your project to find what you anticipate will affect your later aims. You are testing a hypothesis, and it is always possible that you will be wrong. That is not a sin, it just falsifies the hypothesis. However, if you have constructed your project so that later aims depend upon a certain result in the earlier aim, you may have blown up the rationale for the rest of your project. This can be disastrous, and can lead to the reviewer rejecting the entire proposal. Thus, it is important to avoid, wherever, possible, having one aim dependent upon the outcome of a previous aim (unless there is

Clifford B. Saper, MD, PhD

something to test productively regardless of how that aim came out). And if you do have dependent aims, you have to use the Potential Problems and Pitfalls to address how you will handle the situation. In our example, the second Specific Aim may have been to retest the subjects after successful treatment with CPAP to show that they have not improved (i.e., the damage is permanent). Even if the first Aim found no difference, you still may want to do this, as it is possible that after CPAP treatment the subjects with lower levels of hypoxemia, who initially were hung over the next day from poor sleep but not after two weeks of CPAP treatment, may improve, while the patients with hypoxemia greater than hypercarbia may not. But you have to explain the reason why you would want to go on with the second test, even if the first one fails.

REVISION AND RESUBMISSION

Of course, no one likes to think that the proposal that they have just slaved over for weeks on end may end up in the unfunded pile. However, with NIH pay lines for grants between 10-25 percentile, it is clear that at least three-quarters of them will suffer that fate.

The first thing to realize is that this process is *not* personal. The reviewer is just trying to his or her job. You should not take anything away from the process about individuals who may have been reviewers, as quite often the author of the proposal is incorrect in guessing who may have supported their proposal or been critical of it. You also have to grow a very thick skin, as rejection is always painful. Experienced investigators still feel emotional responses when their proposals are turned down (and virtually every investigator now goes through this from time to time). Typically, the feelings follow the well known progression for any type of loss: denial, anger, depression, and eventually, acceptance. You should not try to deal with the situation until you have entered the last phase, and so it is often necessary to put the review away for a few days or even weeks before going back to it, and reconsidering what you can do to respond to the criticisms.

When you can deal with the situation without emotion, you should analyze what the reviewers are actually asking for. If the proposal is on the borderline for funding, and the criticisms can be dealt with by text revision, it is sometimes possible to turn the proposal around for the next resubmission date.

However, in many cases the reviewers want more preliminary data, or substantial restructuring of the proposal. Some investigators are tempted to put in a *rebuttal* letter, indicating why the requests by the reviewers are unreasonable. This can be put in for the next cycle, and there is the possibility that perhaps your original proposal can still be funded. Rebuttals rarely succeed. The reason is that you are making the case for the reviewer's lapse to the same study section that made the original decision. That reviewer is in the room to defend himself or herself, but you are not. This is a very lopsided battle, and the investigator always loses. In addition, you will incite the very study section that you need to approve your application on the next round. Don't do it.

Once you have decided to write a resubmission that requires substantive change, take the time that is necessary to do this properly. With the new NIH rules, this is your last chance for funding that proposal. You should identify exactly what is needed to comply with the reviewers, map out a strategy to provide that information or revision, and do it. If your revised application is really responsive to the reviewers, your chances of funding will be dramatically increased.

The body of the proposal may be preceded by up to two pages of Introduction, in which you can respond to the reviewers. No matter how off-base some of the comments may seem to you, no matter how upset you are with them, you should always begin by thanking the reviewers for their constructive criticisms, and explain that you have tried to incorporate all of their suggestions, and that you believe this has strengthened the proposal. Remember that the reviewers have spent a lot of their own time on *your* work, and they do not get credit for this as co-authors, and they are not paid for it. A harsh response by the investigator will not win your proposal any friends. You should make sure that the tone of your response indicates gratefulness to the reviewers.

You should then work through the criticism, one by one, with each one getting a separate paragraph. Indicate how you have changed the application, and in what pages or sections or figures The application itself should have these changes marked. A good way to do this is with the Word Tracking Tool, by using only the line in the margin to indicate changes. Make it easy for the reviewer to find the changes and nod that you have done exactly what they asked you to do.

Finally, what should you do if, after two rounds you are not funded, and do not have the opportunity to reapply? If you still think that your ideas are good ones, you may be able to repackage at least some of them in a different form, and perhaps submit a somewhat different new proposal. Discuss this with your Program Director. Perhaps a different spin on things will help direct the project to a different study section which may be more sympathetic. The most important thing to learn is persistence. You will not be funded 100% of the time on proposals you do not submit.

Chapter VIII

Developing Grant Budgets:
How to Get What You Need

Phyllis C. Zee, MD, PhD

Introduction

The budget of a grant is one of the most important core components of any grant application, because if you don't get what you need, you will not be able to accomplish the aims of the proposed research. The budget should be determined by the science that is being proposed because it is not used to assess scientific merit, but the budget does reveal how the applicant understands the resources needed to accomplish the science that is being proposed. A lean budget will not rescue a mediocre project; and if inadequate, it could actually hinder the overall merit of the application by raising a concern regarding feasibility. Thus, it is important to develop a realistic budget based on the science and justify your needs in detail.

Before preparing a detailed budget, first, get an overall estimate of what your personnel, equipment and operating costs, and then identify agencies to fund your project and the mechanisms of support, such as the type of grant (R01, R21, K- series awards) or whether you are applying in response to a Program Announcement (PA) or Request for Application (RFA). This will determine budget maximums and allowable costs and the type of support mechanism that is appropriate for your project. Furthermore, specific budget requirements will vary by funding agency and grant mechanism, even within a single institution, such as the National Institutes of Health (NIH) and its specific institutes.

As early as possible, involve your department administrator, who can help you develop your budget and ensure that it complies with the policies of your local institution, such as rates for indirect costs to help guide your application through the process for approval and signatures. Typically your application, but in particular the budget, will need to be processed through your Division, Department and the Office of Research and Sponsored Projects (ORSP) or your institution's grants and contracts management group. Therefore, allow sufficient time for each of these partners to review your budget.

This chapter will provide a general guideline, as well as specific instructions and helpful tips for developing a research grant budget for NIH grants. Examples of the more common types of NIH grant mechanisms, such as R01, R21 and K series awards will used to illustrate these points. Although the focus will be on NIH budgets, many of the same general principles described in this chapter also applies to other funding agencies.

Developing Your Budget

As you begin to plan a budget for the research plan, list all of the applicable costs within the following major categories: (a) Personnel (labor, intellectual effort); (b) Equipment/Instrumentation; (c) Operating costs (patient/subject/ animal care costs, supplies, subcontracts, consultants); and (d) Travel. Then identify the specific budget requirements for your application, such as total costs (does this include both direct and indirect costs?); allowance for investigator salary and benefits, facilities and administration (F&A) cost, etc., to determine how to structure and work within the limitation of these budgetary restrictions. Example of a Budget and Budget Justification for an R01 is provided in **Figures 1 and 2**.

MODULAR VS. NON-MODULAR BUDGET

An NIH R01 grant may be submitted with a modular or non-modular budget. If the total direct cost of the project is $250,000 or less, a modular budget may be used. Each module is $25,000 and you can have increments up to a maximum of $250,000. Therefore, if your direct cost is $250,000 or less, and you are applying for an R01, R21, R03, R15 and the applicant organization is based in the United States, a modular format can be used. Although for modular grants, a detailed budget is not submitted to the NIH, a Budget Justification section is required. In addition, an itemized budget for each of the sections that will be described in this chapter is required by your business office and ORSP for internal budgeting purposes and approval. Remember that modular grants are not adjustable for inflation.

It is also important to consider that although there is no limit to the requested direct costs for an R01 application, applications requesting direct costs of $500,000 or more in any year of the grant period per year must contact the NIH and obtain approval prior to submission.

TOTAL COST = DIRECT + INDIRECT COSTS

Direct costs are research expenses that are allowable and are specifically and directly attributed to the conduct of the project and are specified in the proposal budget. These costs must be allowable, allocable and reasonable according to the guidelines of the funding agency and the sponsoring institution. Typically direct costs include, but not limited to, personnel, consultants, equipment, supplies, travel, participant or animal care costs. Whereas indirect costs, often referred to as "overhead" is also known as financial & administrative (F&A) expenses are those costs incurred by the research institution for common objectives. The F&A rate (indirect cost rate) is used to distribute or compensate the research institution for commonly incurred costs for sponsored research activities. The F&A rate is negotiated by the university or other research entity with the funding agency, such as NIH, foundation or industry. For example, some foundations do not allow indirect cost. Therefore, each institution may have a different F&A rate for the different agencies (NIH, foundations, industry) as well as for the various types of grant mechanisms. (Table 1) Because rates change over time and, not all direct costs are subject to a F&A rate, it is important to consult with your institution's ORSP. Some examples of indirect cost include building use, equipment depreciation, operation and maintenance of the research facility, departmental administration and other administrative support units of a university or research institution.

The actual indirect cost of a specific grant application in universities and most research institutions is calculated using the Modified Total Direct Costs (MTDC) base. MTDC exclude certain categories from being included in the direct costs that indirect cost rate are applied against. In general MTDC consists of personnel salaries and fringe benefits, supplies and travel. Excluded from the MTDC base are equipment, participant support costs and patient care costs. In most cases, once you have developed the budget for your direct costs, the Departmental administrator or ORSP official will determine what goes into the MTDC.

PERSONNEL AND SALARIES

Personnel costs will generally be the largest expense category, accounting for approximately 60-70 percent of the entire budget. Be realistic about what each individual can accomplish and the time necessary to complete the work. For example, if the project requires overnight or 24 hour measurements, such as is often the case in sleep research, one may need to budget for an additional 50 percent technician to be in compliance with local guidelines on extended work hours.

Personnel includes principal investigator, co-investigators, technicians, research coordinators, postdoctoral fellows, graduate students and undergraduate students. Generally, secretarial and clerical support for the investigators or research program is not allowed. Only under certain circumstances and

Table 1 Example of Facilities and Administrative (F&A) Rates at a University

Federal Projects	Fiscal 2009 (9/1/08-8/31/09)	Fiscal 2010 (9/1/09-8/31/10)	Fiscal 2011 (9/1/10-8/31/11)
Sponsored Research – on campus	52.5%	52.5%	52.5%
DoD Contracts – on campus	53.5%	53.5%	53.5%
Other Sponsored Activity – on campus	36.0%	36.0%	36.0%
Sponsored Instruction – on campus	51.0% MTDC*	51.0% MTDC*	51.0% MTDC*
All Programs – off campus	26.0% MTDC*	26.0% MTDC*	26.0% MTDC*

Non-Federal Projects	FY09 & Future Years On-Campus Rate/Base	FY09 & Future Years Off-Campus Rate/Base
Sponsored Research	64.4% MTDC*	33.3% MTDC*
Other Sponsored Activity	44.9% MTDC*	34.8% MTDC*
Sponsored Instruction/Training	89.1% MTDC*	60.7% MTDC*
Industry Clinical Trials	26.0% TDC**	26.0% TDC**

*Modified Total Direct Cost (MTDC)
**Total Direct Cost (TDC)

depending on the type of award mechanism or program announcement would secretarial staff be allowed in the personnel cost. Salaries and wages should be budgeted commensurate with the level of effort required for each person and clearly justified in the Budget Justification section. Determine the type and number of personnel and the amount of time (effort) that investigators and staff will spend on the project during the academic or calendar year or summer months. Whether summer salary is allowed will depend on the type of appointment. For example, if a person's salary is based on a 12-month appointment, supplemental summer salary is not allowed, whereas, another person whose salary is based on an academic year of 9 months, summer salary may be requested if that individual will be spending effort on the project during the summer months.

Factor in current salaries and anticipated increases. Typically salaries and wages should be increased by 3 percent for each succeeding budget period. For NIH grants, there is a salary cap ($19 ,300 for 2009). In addition to the actual salary, fringe benefit rate is also part of the direct cost. Fringe benefit rate is calculated on a fiscal year basis and will vary among institutions and the type of appointment. Therefore, it is important to consult ORSP to determine the current and also anticipated changes in benefit rate over the grant period.

Phyllis C. Zee, MD, PhD

CONSULTANT COSTS

In addition to personnel, projects may require consultants whose expertise is needed for the project. Provide names and institutional affiliation and indicate fees to be paid. Consultants who are employees of the applicant's institution are allowed to serve in this capacity, but may not be allowed to receive payment for these services. Consultant fee is usually determined by the number of hours of service at a rate that is reasonable and justifiable. Note that travel costs requested for consultants should be budgeted here and NOT in the Travel category.

EQUIPMENT

Equipment is defined as instrumentation or technology with a cost of $5,000 or more and have a useful life of more than one year. This can be in the form of a single piece of equipment or may be multiple purchases for different parts, each of less than $5,000, but together cost $5,000 or more to form single system. The latter may be particularly relevant to sleep research, where recording systems need to be assembled for the simultaneous measurement of multiple physiological variables during sleep and wake states. Equipment should be specific for the research project and is usually requested during year 1 of the grant. Because of the typically high cost of equipment, any request for equipment will be scrutinized and thus should be accompanied by a written justification. In modular budget format, you may be able to ask for extra module to cover the cost of major equipment. Equipment is excluded from indirect cost calculations.

SUPPLIES

Supplies consist of instrumentation or items that cost less than $5,000 or have a useful life of less than one year. Supplies have to be directly allocable to the research project. For example, "supplies" does not include general office supplies. Supplies are subject to indirect costs. The following are examples of categories of items that are allowable:

Research/Lab Supplies: Chemicals, medical and surgical supplies (glassware, batteries, EEG electrodes) etc.
Research Equipment: Microscopes, appliances, instruments, etc.
Office Equipment/Furniture: Fax machines, telephones, calculators, printer stands, etc.
Computer: Desktop personal computers, laptop computers, modems, printers
Experimental Animals: Live animals used for research project
Printing: Paper, toner, questionnaires, etc.
Other Supplies: Drugs, shipping supplies

TRAVEL

This component is typically small, approximately $1,000 per individual (usually 2-3 investigators) per year for transportation, lodging and other related travel costs necessary to conduct the research project or attend a professional meeting for individuals listed under "Personnel." If foreign travel is necessary, it must be separately described and justified from the domestic costs. Note that travel costs for consultants should not be listed in this category. If research assistants will need to travel to participants homes, for example, mileage reimbursement should also be listed in this section, and carefully justified with the per mile cost.

PATIENT CARE COSTS

For patient oriented research and clinical trials, patient care costs can be divided into "usual patient care" (costs incurred even if the patient was not participating in the research) and "research patient care" costs of medical services provided by a hospital or clinic for the purpose of research only to the research participant. The budget should only request funds for "research patient care" costs, such as routine and ancillary services provided to patients participating in the research project. For sleep research projects, this may include polysomnography, blood work, electrocardiogram, etc. Patient care costs do not include patient travel or any direct payments to patients, including for compensation of their time. These items should be listed under the Other Expenses category. Patient care costs are based on the rates that have been negotiated between the institution and Healthcare Financial Administration and the Department of Health and Human Services (DHHS). In most institutions, patient care costs are computed in a manner consistent with the principles and procedures used by the Medicare Program for determining the part of Medicare reimbursement based on reasonable costs and patient care rates established by DHHS.

OTHER EXPENSES

The Other Expenses category include all other costs that are required, but do not fall into any of the other categories discussed above. Most of the items in this category are likely to be operational costs. Below is a list and brief description of some of the common subcategories:

Animal Care Services/Per Diem: This subcategory is to be used for all expenses related to animal care such as purchasing, renting, leasing, caring for and disposing of animals.

Information Technology (IT)/Computer Services: This subcategory includes charges for the use of IT support for the computing services, data processing, programming, software and database management services necessary for the proposed research.

Maintenance and Repair of Equipment: It is a good idea to build in the cost of repairs, maintenance and other service agreements into the budget.

Participant or Patient Compensation: This category is to be used to reimburse costs such as participant travel to and from the research institution (mileage, parking); subsistence allowances (food and beverage during the research activity); registration fees to be paid to the participants or trainees. For example, if the project is a study on the effects of exercise on sleep and the exercise will be conducted in an exercise facility, registration for the participant during the active research period may be allowable. It is important to determine which items in this subcategory are allowable by the sponsor and may vary depending on the mechanism of the grant.

Membership Dues: Membership dues for investigators and staff are not allowed.

Postage/Overnight Delivery: Postage can only be charged to a grant if it is specifically identified and justified in the proposal and directly necessary to implement the procedures of the study. For example, the project involves the use of actigraphy and collection of biological samples in the field, and the plan is for the participants to mail these back to you after the collection period, a postage charge would be appropriate. For this subcategory, it is important to check whether prior sponsor approval is required by NIH.

Research Job Related Training/ Professional Development: Costs associated with training or professional development required for the research project or taken to maintain or improve skills required in present work. This may include, but not limited to course work and workshops

Printing and Publishing: The costs of printing, photocopying, photographing incurred in producing material for the research project. Publishing charges are costs incurred for publishing articles of the results of the proposed research. This subcategory should be less than $1,000.

Figure 1

Principal Investigator/Program Director (Last, first, middle):							

DETAILED BUDGET FOR INITIAL BUDGET PERIOD
DIRECT COSTS ONLY

FROM: 12/1/08 THROUGH: 11/30/09

PERSONNEL (Applicant organization only)		Months Devoted to Project				DOLLAR AMOUNT REQUESTED (omit cents)		
NAME	ROLE ON PROJECT	Cal. Mnths	Acad. Mnths	Sum. Mnths	INST. BASE SALARY	SALARY REQUESTED	FRINGE BENEFITS	TOTALS
	Principal Investigator	1.8	15%		$191,300	$28,695	$6,508	$35,203
	Co-PI	1.2	10%		$191,300	$19,130	$4,339	$23,469
	Co-Investigator	0.36	3%		$191,300	$5,739	$1,302	$7,041
	Fellow	4.8	40%		$77,250	$30,900	$7,008	$37,908
	Co-Investigator	1.8	15%		$64,184	$9,628	$2,184	$11,812
	Sleep Tech	7.2	60%		$41,200	$24,720	$5,606	$30,326
	Co-Investigator	0.6	5%		$105,993	$5,300	$1,202	$6,502
	Programmer	2.4	20%		$76,088	$15,218	$3,451	$18,669
	Study coordinator	6	50%		$48,006	$24,003	$5,444	$29,447
	Data Manager	2.4	20%		$106,298	$21,260	$4,822	$26,082
	Clinic manager	0.63	6%	3%	$85,567	$4,492	$1,019	$5,511
	Recruiter	4.2	40%	20%	$43,384	$15,184	$3,444	$18,628
	Health Interviewer	4.2	40%	20%	$46,414	$16,245	$3,684	$19,929
SUBTOTALS ⟶						$220,514	$50,013	$270,527

CONSULTANT COSTS

EQUIPMENT (Itemize)

SUPPLIES (Itemize by category)

Computer supplies		120
PSG supplies		$8,400
FedEx		18,275
Actiwatches (35)		36600
IL-6Assays		2,100
		$65,495

TRAVEL	Travel for investigators to attaned one annual scientific meeting	1200
		$1,200

PATIENT CARE COSTS	INPATIENT
	OUTPATIENT

ALTERATIONS AND RENOVATIONS (Itemize by category)

OTHER EXPENSES (Itemize by category)

Subject compensation	44,950
Subject Parking	5,408
	$50,358

CONSORTIUM/CONTRACTUAL COSTS	DIRECT COSTS	
SUBTOTAL DIRECT COSTS FOR INITIAL BUDGET PE (Item 7a, Face Page)	$	387,580
CONSORTIUM/CONTRACTUAL COSTS	FACILITIES AND ADMINISTRATION COSTS	
TOTAL DIRECT COSTS FOR INITIAL BUDGET PERIOD	$	387,580
SBIR/STTR Only: FEE REQUESTED		

PHS 398 (Rev. 04/06)   Page _____   Form Page 4

Telephone: Only telephone line charges for phones and long distance calls dedicated exclusively to the project are allowable.

Other Services: For clinical research studies, advertising and recruitment costs can also be included in the budget.

An example of the Budget Justification for this category is provided in **Figure 2**.

COST ESCALATION

The budget represents your best estimation of the cost of the proposed research for year 1 and the total years of the project. Depending on the award mechanism, the total project period may be 2 years (for an R21) or up to 5 years (for an R01) or longer for NIH contracts. It is not expected that your budget will exactly reflect how the funds will be spent over the next 3-5 years. However, it is important to be able to convince the reviewers that your approximation of what you plan to spend is in accordance with the propose work and that you have made the necessary adjustments for change in intensity of procedures, equipment, supplies, and personnel effort during each of the years.

In the budget, you may request an escalation factor for recurring costs in compliance with your institution's and funding institution's policies. For example, the NIH will generally allow up to a 3 percent increase each year for recurring costs, such as salaries and supplies. However, the adjustment on salaries cannot exceed the NIH cap on salaries for that year. Prior to factoring in a cost escalation rate, it is prudent to consult the NIH appropriation for the specific fiscal year. (see NIH Guide Notice NOT-OD-09-066). An example of the budget for the entire project period is shown in **Figure 2**.

Beyond the customary increase in living expenses, any large year-to-year change should be described in your budget justification. For example, if you anticipate a substantial increase in the effort of a biostatistician in the final year of the project, a clear explanation for this increase in effort is required in the Budget Justification section. Generally, the cost of equipment and major supplies are budgeted during year one and replacement supplies over the ensuing years. However, if a piece of equipment for analysis is not required until year three, it makes sense to purchase then, and should be justified in the year three budget.

POST AWARD CHANGES IN BUDGET AND NO-COST EXTENSION

Recognizing that adjustments in cost and expenditures will be required over the grant period, NIH grantees are allowed some latitude to re-distribute money between the various budget categories to meet necessary unanticipated changes, such as changes in personnel. If the changes are minor and in compliance with the sponsoring institution's policy and within the limits established by NIH, prior approval from the NIH is not needed. Under the "Expanded Authorities" guidelines established by NIH, carryover of unobligated balances of 25 percent or less of the total budget from one budget period to the next including patient care costs, supplies and equipment and extension of the final budget period without additional NIH funds for up to 12 months do not require NIH pre-approval. However, the grantee must notify the NIH awarding office, in writing, of the extension at least 10 days prior to the expiration date of the project period. In other cases, such as when there is a significant change in the effort of key personnel, change in the scope of the project, or no-cost extension beyond 12 months prior approval must be obtained from the NIH or other funding agencies before any modifications can be made.

(See NIH Grants Policy Statement - Changes in Project and Budget)

Phyllis C. Zee, MD, PhD

Figure 2

Principal Investigator/Program Director (Last, first, middle): _____

BUDGET FOR ENTIRE PROPOSED PERIOD OF SUPPORT
DIRECT COSTS ONLY

BUDGET CATEGORY TOTALS		INITIAL BUDGET PERIOD (from Form Page 4)	ADDITIONAL YEARS OF SUPPORT REQUESTED			
			2nd	3rd	4th	5th
PERSONNEL: *Salary and fringe benefits. Applicant organization only.*		$270,527	$267,187	$307,966	$261,109	
CONSULTANT COSTS						
EQUIPMENT						
SUPPLIES		$65,495	$37,545	$16,370		
TRAVEL		$1,200	$2,400	$2,400	$4,800	
PATIENT CARE COSTS	INPATIENT					
	OUTPATIENT					
ALTERATIONS AND RENOVATIONS						
OTHER EXPENSES		$50,358	$39,154	$17,704	$3,000	
CONSORTIUM/ CONTRACTUAL COSTS	DIRECT					
SUBTOTAL DIRECT COSTS *(Sum = Item 8a, Face Page)*		$387,580	$346,286	$344,440	$268,909	
CONSORTIUM/ CONTRACTUAL COSTS	F&A					
TOTAL DIRECT COSTS		$387,580	$346,286	$344,440	$268,909	
TOTAL DIRECT COSTS FOR ENTIRE PROPOSED PERIOD OF SUPPORT						$1,347,215

JUSTIFICATION. Follow the budget justification instructions exactly. Use continuation pages as needed.

BUDGET JUSTIFICATION

The success of this project relies on the close collaboration of an interdisciplinary team of investigators and staff from sleep medicine and preventive medicine. The requested budget covers both the clinic visit in the Department of Preventive Medicine Clinic, as well as the laboratory component in which physiological sleep and neuropsychological assessments will be performed in the General Clinical Research Center (GCRC) in the subset of 150 participants.

Personnel

Name of Investigator: Professor of Neurology and Director of the Sleep Disorders Center will serve as the first Principal Investigator and Contact PI of this project. Dr XX has been conducting research in the area of sleep and circadian rhythms for over 15 years. Working in close collaboration with Dr. XY, Dr. XX will be responsible for overseeing the coordination of all of the phases of the proposed study with the Parent study, including protocol development, recruitment, ensuring study integrity and the preparation of presentations and manuscripts. In addition, she will direct the design and experimental procedures and data analysis of the physiological sleep and neuropsychological assessments. Dr. XX will devote 1.8 calendar months each year to this project.

Name of Investigator, Professor of Preventive Medicine and Medicine (Geriatrics) serves as the second Principal Investigator of this project. Dr XY has been conducting research on CV and nutritional epidemiology and working on

Figure 2 continued on following page

Figure 2 *(continued)*

studies involving for more than 10 years. In close collaboration with Dr. XX, Dr. XY will be responsible for overseeing the coordination of both projects, participate in protocol development, and in preparation of presentations and publications. She will devote 1.2 calendar months each year to this project.

Name of Investigator, Professor of Preventive Medicine serves as a Co-Investigator of this project. He has been involved on research projects utilizing data from large cohorts for over 20 years and has been working closely with Dr. XY on several studies, including the one proposed in this Study, for more than 10 years. As Co-Investigator he will provide input and expertise in the methodology and the statistical analyses of the study data. Dr. XZ will devote 0.36 calendar months each year to this project in Years 1-3 and 0.6 calendar months in Year 4.

Name of Investigator, Research Assistant Professor of Neurology serves as a Co-Investigator of this project. Dr XYZ will be responsible for the day-to-day supervision of all the study procedures and for the physiological and sleep studies conducted at the General Clinical Research Center (GCRC). Dr XYZ will also be responsible for the analyses and interpretation of the neurobehavioral performance and sleep data (wrist activity and PSG). In addition, she will participate in presentation of data and publication of manuscripts. Dr XYZ will devote 1.8 calendar months each year to this project.

Name of Investigator, Assistant Professor of Preventive Medicine serves as a Co-Investigator of this project. Dr XXX is highly experienced in conducting biostatistics methodological research on area of survival analysis, semi-parametric modeling, resampling methods, and model checking and evaluation methods. Dr. XXX also has interest in computational biology. He will provide statistical expertise to the study, particularly in the area of informative censoring. Dr XXX will devote 0.6 calendar months to this project in Year 1, 1.2 calendar months in Year 2, and 2.4 calendar months each year in Years 3-4.

Name of investigator, Instructor of Neurology and Medicine will devote 4.8 calendar months to this project in Years 1-3 and 3.6 calendar months in Year 4. Dr BL will conduct history and physical examinations in the subgroup of 150 CHA participants taking part in the sleep lab component at the GCRC. He will also be responsible for scoring and reading the PSG studies.

Programmer, Statistical Analyst/Programmer has considerable expertise in dataset preparation and analysis. Ms. Chan has participated in the preparation of numerous abstracts, presentations, and manuscripts. She will continue in this capacity and devote 2.4 calendar months each year to this project in Years 1-2 and 6 calendar months each year in Years 3-4.

Research Program Manager, Research Programming Manager for the Department of Preventive Medicine will serve as Data Manager and Senior Programmer for this project. In this capacity he will be responsible for maintaining the databases for the cohorts, for ongoing processing, and for interim quality control reporting. He will be responsible for the design and implementation of participant tracking and data acquisition systems. He has had over 20 years of experience with research databases and data management of the CHA cohorts. Mr. DG will devote 2.4 calendar months each year to this project in Year 1-4.

Research Coordinator, Research Study Coordinator will devote 6 calendar months to this project in Year 1-3 and 2.4 calendar months in Year 4. She will schedule participants, organize transportation for the GCRC physiological and sleep lab component. She will also conduct testing procedure on day 2 of the GCRC lab component and coordinate transfer of samples for analysis. In addition she will be responsible for initial analyses and data entry of the sleep variables obtained from the 1,380 participants, i.e., 4140 days of sleep log and wrist activity monitoring.

Clinic Manager, Clinic Manager, will devote 0.63 calendar months to this project in Year 1. In Year 2 and 3 she will devote 0.36 calendar months each year to this project. The increased effort in Year 1 will allow her to conduct interviews for the 331 participants that will need to be brought back to complete the sleep ancillary. She will be responsible for supervising all day-to-day clinic activities and clinic staff.

Health Interviewer, Health Interviewer, will devote 4.2 calendar months of her time to this project in Year 1. In Year 2 she will devote 2.4 calendar months to this project and in Year 3, she will devote 0.6 calendar months. The increased effort in Year 1 will allow her to conduct interviews for the 331 participants that will need to be bought back to complete the sleep ancillary. She will review the inform consent with participants, conduct interviews, check questionnaires for completeness, and provide instructions for the wrist activity monitor and sleep diary. She will also be responsible for, copying forms and assembling questionnaire packages.

Recruiter, Recruiter, will devote 4.2 calendar months to this project in Year 1. In Year 2 and 3 she will devote 2.4 calendar months each year to this project. The increased effort in Year 1 will allow her to recruit the 331 participants that will need

Figure 2 continued on following page

Figure 2 *(continued)*

to be bought back to complete the sleep ancillary. She will be responsible for participant recruitment, scheduling of appointments for examination, arranging transportation when required, and sending materials to participants

Research Technician, Sleep technician/research assistant will devote 7.2 calendar months of her time to this project in Year 1-3. In Year 4 she will devote 3.75 calendar months of her time to this project. She will score and enter data for the 300 nocturnal polysomnographic (PSG) sleep studies and for the 750 Multiple Sleep Latency Tests obtained from 150 participants. She will conduct EEG spectral analyses and data entry. She will also assist with data scanning and editing and with the initial analyses and data entry of the sleep variables obtained from the 1,380 participants, i.e., 4140 days of sleep log and wrist activity monitoring.

Annual salary increases. Salaries are increased by 3% per year.

Employee benefits. "Employee benefits have been calculated based on the following DHHS approved rates: 9/1/08 – 8/31/09 .... 22.50% (estimated), 9/1/09 – 8/31/10 .... 23.20% (estimated), 9/1/10 – 8/31/11 .... 23.50% (estimated), 9/1/11 – 8/31/12 & thereafter.... 23.70% (estimated)

NIH Salary Cap. The following investigators are currently making more than the NIH salary cap: Dr's XX, XZ and XYZ.

Travel

Support is requested for one trip to scientific meetings in Year 1, 2 meetings each year in Years 2 and 3, and 4 trips in Year 4 for the Principal Investigator and other investigators. Each trip is estimated to cost $1,200, with $475 for airfare, $450 for hotel accommodations (two days at $225/day), $175 for registration, and $100 for ground transportation.

Other Direct Costs

Materials and Supplies

Polysomnography (PSG) Supplies: Funds for sleep study supplies are requested, items include; Elefix Paste, alcohol wipes, NuPrep, gauze rolls and squares, cotton swabs, hypoallergenic surgical tape, head wrap, replacement electrodes and data storage media (DVD and CD). It is estimated that the total cost will be $100/night for 300 PSG studies, this includes 750 Multiple Sleep Latency Tests. PSG supplies will be $8,400 in Year 1 and $10,800/year in each of Years 2 and 3.

Computer supplies: Given the large volume of printing (questionnaires, Sleep Log, Informed Consent, Recruitment Letters and Result Letters) we estimate that one toner cartridge will be required in each year, for years 1-3 at $120 each.

Activity monitors: The purchase of thirty-five activity monitors will be required in Year 1, and an additional 10 in Year 2 of the project (to replace lost and broken monitors). In Year 1, $36,600 is requested and in Year 2 $10,450. This price includes twice yearly calibration and battery changes.

Federal Express shipping costs are requested for the return of the activity monitors. Funds are requested to utilize Federal Express to minimize damage/loss to this expensive equipment. It is estimated to cost an average of $25 per package. In year 1, 731 participants will be examined with activity monitors for a cost of $18,275. In year 2, 539 participants at a cost of $13,475 and in year 3, 110 participants at a cost of $2,750.

Assay of Interleukin-6 (IL6): Funds are requested for the assay of IL6. A total of 150 samples will be assayed at a cost of $50/sample for a total of $7,500. In year 1, 42 participants will have IL6 levels determined as part of the GCRC study for a total cost of $2,100. In year 2 and 3, 54 participants each year will have IL6 levels determined as part of the GCRC study for a cost of $2,700/year in Year 2 and 3.

Publication costs. Funds are requested to pay for the costs of artwork for manuscripts, reprints and page charges, photocopying, and for the costs of slides and posters to be used in presentations. The costs are estimated to be $3,000 in Year 4 based on current actual costs for similar work.

Participant compensation. To maximize participation, participants will be compensated for their time and effort completing the study procedures. Participants will be compensated $50/person for completing the questionnaires and sleep log and wearing the activity monitor. In year 1, 731 participants will complete the questionnaire at a cost of $36,550, in year 2, 539 participants at a cost of $26,950 and in year 3, 110 participants at a cost of $5,500. Participants that complete the physiology and sleep study in the GCRC will receive $200/person ($100/night for 2 nights). In year 1, 42

Figure 2 continued on following page

Figure 2 *(continued)*

participants will complete the GCRC study for a total cost of $8,400. In year 2 and 3, 54 participants will complete the GCRC study each year for a cost of $10,800/year in Year 2 and 3. The total cost of participant compensation for the GCRC studies will be $30,000.

Participant parking/transport reimbursement. To maximize participation in the CHAS based sleep study all 331 participants bought back in Year 1 will be reimbursed for public transportation (max. $10.00/visit/person) or parking costs ($16/visit/person). Based on experience with the CHA pilot study, we estimate that approximately half of the participants will drive and half will take public transportation. Public transportation amounts are budgeted for half of the participants (166) who are expected to drive/take public transportation and will be $1660 in Year 1 only. Parking reimbursement amounts are budgeted for the remaining half of participants (166) who will drive and will be $2,656 in Year 1 only. For the physiological study, all 150 participants will be reimbursed for public transportation (max. $10.00/visit/person) or parking costs ($16/visit/person). Public transportation amounts are budgeted for half of the participants (2 visits per participant) who are expected take public transportation based upon 42 visits in Year 1, and 54 visits in each of Years 2 and 3. For a total of $420 for in Year 1, and $540 in each of Years 2 and 3. The total cost for public transportation is $1,500. Parking reimbursement amounts are budgeted for the remaining half of participants expected to drive based upon 42 visits in Year 1, and 54 visits in each of Years 2 and 3. For a cost of $672 in Year 1, and $864 in each of Years 2 and 3.

Summary and Conclusion

Any research project, regardless of funding source, requires a budget. A budget is a realistic estimate of what it will cost to complete a study and is developed by thinking through and identifying the expertise, resources and time necessary for each of the components of implementing the research project. You may not get what you want and may not even get what you need. NIH can administratively reduce your budget. Therefore, it is important to identify all the items in each of the categories that you will realistically need in developing your budget. Although it is important to develop a realistic and as lean as possible of a budget that will allow you to complete the research project, it is as equally important to appreciate that for a reviewer, the budget reveals the experience of the applicant to carry out the project and how well the he (she) understands what it takes to get it done. If the budget is inflated, it will turn reviewers off, and if its not insufficient, the reviewers will question the feasibility of the project. So develop a realistic budget, start the process early by engaging your business and grants administrator, consult the funding agency's requirements and justify your needs. Remember that even though it is obvious and crystal clear to you as to why an item is needed and how it ties in with the scientific aims of the study, you still need to convince the reviewers. It is the science that drives the budget and justification.

Resources

http://grants.nih.gov/grants/funding/phs398/phs398.html

http://grants.nih.gov/grants/funding/modular/modular.htm

http://www.research.northwestern.edu/osr/prop.html

http://research.utmb.edu/osp/budget_prepare.shtm

Phyllis C. Zee, MD, PhD

CHAPTER IX

THE GRANT APPLICATION REVIEW PROCESS

Mark R. Opp, PhD

INTRODUCTION

You spent a considerable amount of time and effort developing a strong application. You have an important question with clear clinical relevance. After conversations with one or more program officers within the National Institutes of Health (NIH) institutes or centers (IC) appropriate for your specific area of research, you have developed related, yet independent, Specific Aims with testable hypotheses. You have obtained critical preliminary data representative of each Specific Aim that demonstrate feasibility and a biological basis for your overall hypotheses, and you have written and polished a complete and balanced application. Finally, and hopefully not at the last minute, you have successfully navigated *grants.gov* and uploaded your application. Now what? For many, particularly junior faculty, the peer-review process is the consummate black-box. What happens from the moment the application is successfully submitted until you are able to access *eRA-Commons* and view the score your application received? In this chapter an overview is provided of the NIH grant application peer-review process, from submission to score, based upon experiences as a funded investigator, a former study section member and frequent *ad hoc* reviewer, discussions with study section chairs and NIH Scientific Review Officers.

THE SUBMISSION

CENTER FOR SCIENTIFIC REVIEW

The Center for Scientific Review (CSR) is the entity responsible for the peer review process for most research and research training applications submitted to NIH. The mission of the CSR is to, "see that NIH grant applications receive fair, independent, expert, and timely reviews – free from inappropriate influences – so NIH can fund the most promising research." Among its multiple tasks, and relevant to this chapter, the CSR serves as the central receipt point for applications, assigns NIH applications to appropriate institutes or centers for funding consideration and also assigns the applications to specific scientific review groups, called Integrated Review Groups (IRG) for review. In a normal year, the CSR will receive about 80,000 applications and will recruit more than 17,000 experts to review the applications for which it is responsible. The CSR has developed online resources that provide greater detail about the submission and peer-review process than is included in this overview chapter. Links to many of these resources are provided in the *Useful Information* section at the end of this chapter.

Upon receipt of your application, one (or more) referral officers of CSR will review your application to determine which NIH IC is best suited to fund the application should it be found to have sufficient merit. In some cases, particularly if the principal investigator (PI) specifically requests it (see later), the application will be assigned to as many as three different ICs. At this stage of processing, the CSR referral officer(s) will also determine the most appropriate IRG and study section for review of the application. The CSR referral officers follow guidelines when making assignments that are based upon established review boundaries for each study section. Currently, there are 25 IRGs within CSR, and each IRG is composed of multiple study sections. For example, many applications that focus on basic sleep research are assigned to the Integrated, Functional, and Cognitive Neuroscience (IFCN) IRG. IFCN at present consists of 11 study sections, including the Biological Rhythms and Sleep (BRS) and the

Neuroendocrinology, Neuroimmunology and Behavior (NNB) study sections, to which applications that focus on sleep are often assigned. Another study section to which more clinically-relevant applications are sometimes assigned is the Neural Basis of Psychopathology, Addictions and Sleep Disorders (NPAS) within the Brain Disorders and Clinical Neuroscience (BDCN) IRG. A complete listing of CSR IRGs and study section descriptions is found online (http://cms.csr.nih.gov/peerreviewmeetings/ csrirgdescriptionnew/). Junior faculty and new investigators are encouraged to talk with funded senior PIs, program officers at NIH and others to determine IRGs and study sections that possess expertise relevant to the application being submitted.

THE COVER LETTER

One required component of the *grants.gov* application submission is the cover letter. Junior faculty and new investigators may not be aware that specific requests with respect to IC, IRG, and study section assignment may be made in the cover letter. As a PI it is important that you explicitly, concisely, and politely state your requests with respect to assignment of the application. CSR gives serious consideration to such requests, although referral officers are not obligated to honor them. There are several reasons why it is important to indicate your wishes to CSR. First, you have spent time speaking with program officers of relevant ICs prior to submitting the application so you know which ICs have an interest in adding your proposal to their portfolio. Discussions with IC program officers will provide you with a very good indication as to how your proposed study fits (or not) with the overall mission of a given IC. Referral officer(s) at CSR will not be aware of these discussions, and may not ascertain from a quick review of your application the critical features of the proposal that would make it more (or less) suitable for assignment to one or another of the 27 NIH ICs. It is important to be able judge the degree of interest by a particular IC in your application (by speaking before submission with program officers) and to convey that information to CSR, so your application does not suffer from lack of interest by an IC when final funding decisions are being made.

As previously stated, junior faculty and new investigators should speak with senior PIs with respect to requesting IC assignment. After consultation with others, it is likely you will decide that your proposed study would fit within the mission of more than one NIH IC. A second facet of requests included in the cover letter should be for a dual, or triple, IC assignment. One IC will be designated as the primary IC for the assignment and the others will be simply listed. Budgets and emphasis on/investment in sleep research differ across ICs such that after review your application may be transferred to one or the other of the alternate ICs for funding.

In addition to requesting IC assignments in the cover letter, it is also important to make suggestions with respect to the specific IRG and study section that you think will be the most appropriate to review your application. Although there are review boundaries that guide CSR referral officers in making decisions with respect to IRG and study section assignments, these boundaries frequently (in fact, invariably) overlap to some extent, and more than one study section may have the expertise to review your application. Study section rosters are posted (http://www.drg.nih.gov/Roster_proto/sectionI.asp), and it is in your best interest as a grant applicant to know who are the permanent members of the study section. Such information is critical so you can determine if, in your opinion, appropriate expertise exists to review your application. Given the breadth and the multitude of techniques and approaches used to address questions that cover a broad spectrum of research, it is not likely that expertise will exist among permanent members of the study section to review all applications submitted. If this is indeed determined to be the case, individuals who are not permanent members of the study section will be invited to serve as *ad hoc* reviewers (see later). These *ad hoc* reviewers will also be identified on the study section rosters.

There is one final type of request that may be made in the cover letter, but one for which careful consideration should be given. As an applicant, you may be of the opinion that some specific individual may have an inherent philosophic difference that would preclude an impartial review of your proposal. You may politely state such in your cover letter, but be advised that many factors are considered when the Scientific Review Officer (SRO, see later) decides who among the members of the study section, or potential *ad hoc* reviewers, will be assigned your application. It cannot be emphasized enough that requests to exclude from the potential reviewers of your application individuals with whom you have philosophical differences should be made with utmost respect and courtesy. Keep in mind that the SRO is under no obligation to honor such a request, but for a variety of reasons is likely to do so.

Upon successful submission of your application through *grants.gov* you will be notified by e-mail and by notices posted in your *eRA-Commons* account that the application has been received. You will be notified when your application has been assigned to an IC and study section. The process of assignment by CSR referral officers may take several weeks given the number of applications received. CSR suggests that if a notice is not posted in your *eRA-Commons* account within three (3) weeks that you contact the referral office at (301) 435-0715. Questions about your application during the submission and assignment process should be directed to CSR. Similarly, if after you receive the IC and study section assignments you have questions, or think your application has been assigned to a study section lacking requisite expertise, you should speak with the CSR referral office. After IC and study section assignment, questions should be directed to the SRO, who will be named (with contact information) on your *eRA-Commons* account.

SUPPLEMENTAL MATERIALS

Although one of CSR's initiatives is to streamline and shorten the review process, several months pass from the date of submission until the study section convenes and your application is formally reviewed. During this interval from submission to review, investigators may well continue to work on aspects of the project and may continue to generate data that are relevant to the submitted application. It is possible to submit supplemental information in support of your application after submission and prior to study section review. In addition to additional preliminary date, several types of information may be provided as a supplement to your application. For example, you may have learned that a submitted manuscript relevant to the application has been accepted for publication and wish to inform the reviewers. More generally however, supplemental information takes the form of additional preliminary data.

It is important that you discuss your plans with the SRO before you submit supplemental information. Your SRO will indicate the limitations for your proposed supplement. There are several considerations to keep in mind when deciding whether or not to submit supplemental information. First, the supplement will be submitted directly to the SRO, and must be done so with enough time for the information to be forwarded to the reviewers assigned to your application. The SRO will indicate by what date s/he will need to receive the information, but it is likely to be a minimum of two weeks prior to the study section meeting date. Second, submission of supplemental information *may* annoy the reviewers. Keep in mind the reviewers will have applications to review other than yours, and depending on the number of applications to which they have been assigned their workload may already be heavy. Receiving additional information to review at the last minute may be perceived as more work, and result in the reviewers not giving it as much attention as you may think it deserves. With the impact on the reviewers in mind, every effort should be made to keep the supplement to one (1) page in length. If additional preliminary data are included in the supplement, there should be a brief explanation of the contribution these data make to one or more of the hypotheses and Specific Aims of the submitted application. A graphical representation of the data will have more impact, be easier for the reviewers to assimilate and is less likely to be considered an annoyance by the reviewers than if simply another page of text is provided. Also, although your SRO will likely have informed you during your discussions, the supplement is not to be used as a method to circumvent the page limitations of the overall application.

THE REVIEW

Reviewers are asked to assess your application with respect to each of five review criteria to determine scientific and technical merit. Each of the review criteria, as well as the overall impact and priority, is assigned a separate score (see later). The following descriptions of the review criteria are taken from information provided to study section members (or to *ad hoc* reviewers) when they are asked to review an application.

Overall Impact/Priority NIH peer reviewers are asked to provide an overall impact/priority score to reflect their assessment of the likelihood for the project to exert a sustained, powerful influence on the research field(s) involved, in consideration of the following five core review criteria, and the additional review criteria (as applicable for the project proposed).

Significance Does the project address an important problem or a critical barrier to progress in the field? If the aims of the project are achieved, how will scientific knowledge, technical capability, and/or clinical practice be improved? How will successful completion of the aims change the concepts, methods, technologies, treatments, services, or preventative interventions that drive this field?

Investigator(s) Are the program directors/principal investigators (PD/PIs), collaborators, and other researchers well suited to the project? If Early Stage Investigators or New Investigators, do they have appropriate experience and training? If established, have they demonstrated an ongoing record of accomplishments that have advanced their field(s)? If the project is collaborative or multi-PD/PI, do the investigators have complementary and integrated expertise; are their leadership approach, governance and organizational structure appropriate for the project?

Innovation Does the application challenge and seek to shift current research or clinical practice paradigms by utilizing novel theoretical concepts, approaches or methodologies, instrumentation, or interventions? Are the concepts, approaches or methodologies, instrumentation, or interventions novel to one field of research or novel in a broad sense? Is a refinement, improvement, or new application of theoretical concepts, approaches or methodologies, instrumentation, or interventions proposed?

Approach Are the overall strategy, methodology, and analyses well-reasoned and appropriate to accomplish the specific aims of the project? Are potential problems, alternative strategies, and benchmarks for success presented? If the project is in the early stages of development, will the strategy establish feasibility and will particularly risky aspects be managed? If the project involves clinical research, are the plans for: (1) protection of human subjects from research risks, and (2) inclusion of minorities and members of both sexes/genders, as well as the inclusion of children, justified in terms of the scientific goals and research strategy proposed?

Environment Will the scientific environment in which the work will be done contribute to the probability of success? Are the institutional support, equipment and other physical resources available to the investigators adequate for the project proposed? Will the project benefit from unique features of the scientific environment, subject populations, or collaborative arrangements.

In addition to the five core review criteria, reviewers are asked to consider additional items in the determination of scientific and technical merit, but not to give separate scores for these items. These additional items generally pertain to regulatory compliance issues, such as the use of vertebrate animals or human subjects in your research, among others. As with the core review criteria summarized earlier, the following descriptions are from information provided by CSR to reviewers prior to review of applications.

Protections for Human Subjects For research that involves human subjects but does not involve one of the six categories of research that are exempt under 45 CFR Part 46, reviewers are asked to evaluate the justification for involvement of human subjects and the proposed protections from research risk relating to their participation according to the following five review criteria: (1) risk to subjects, (2) adequacy of protection against risks, (3) potential benefits to the subjects and others, (4) importance of the knowledge to be gained, and (5) data and safety monitoring for clinical trials. If all of the criteria are adequately addressed, and there are no concerns, write "Acceptable Risks and/or Adequate Protections." A brief explanation is advisable. If one or more criteria are inadequately addressed, write, "Unacceptable Risks and/or Inadequate Protections" and document the actual or potential issues that create the human subjects concern. Also, if a clinical trial is proposed, evaluate the Data and Safety Monitoring Plan. (If the plan is absent, notify the SRO immediately to determine if the application should be withdrawn.) Indicate if the plan is "Acceptable" or "Unacceptable," and, if unacceptable, explain why it is unacceptable. For research that involves human subjects and meets the criteria for one or more of the six categories of research that are exempt, evaluate: (1) the justification for the exemption, (2) human subjects involvement and characteristics, and (3) sources of materials. If the claimed exemption is not justified, indicate "Unacceptable," and, if unacceptable, explain why it is unacceptable. *NOTE: To the degree that acceptability or unacceptability affects the investigator's approach to the proposed research, such comments should appear under "Approach" in the five major review criteria above, and should be factored into the score as appropriate.* For additional information to assist you in making these determinations, please refer to http://grants.nih.gov/grants/peer/guidelines_general/Human_Subjects_Protection_and_Inclusion_a5.pdf and http://grants.nih.gov/grants/peer/guidelines_general/Human_Subjects_Worksheet_a5.pdf.

Inclusion of Women, Minorities and Children When the proposed project involves clinical research, reviewers are asked to evaluate the proposed plans for inclusion of minorities and members of both genders, as well as the inclusion of children. Public Law 103-43 requires that women and minorities must be included in all NIH-supported clinical research projects involving human subjects unless a clear and compelling rationale establishes that inclusion is inappropriate with respect to the health of the subjects or the purpose of the research. NIH requires that children (individuals under the age of 21) of all ages be involved in all human subjects research supported by the NIH unless there are scientific or ethical reasons for excluding them. Each project involving human subjects must be assigned a code using the categories "1" to "5" below. Category 5 for minority representation in the project means that only foreign subjects are in the study population (no U.S. subjects). If the study uses both then use codes 1 thru 4. Examine whether the minority and gender characteristics of the sample are scientifically acceptable, consistent with the aims of the project, and comply with NIH policy. For each category, determine if the proposed subject recruitment targets are "A" (acceptable) or "U" (unacceptable). If you rate the sample as "U", consider this feature a weakness in the research design and reflect it in the overall score. Explain the reasons for the recommended codes; this is particularly critical for any item coded "U". *NOTE: To the degree that acceptability or unacceptability affects the investigator's approach to the proposed research, such comments should appear under "Approach" in the five major review criteria above, and should be factored into the score as appropriate.*

Mark R. Opp, PhD

Table 1 Nine-point scoring system adopted by the Center for Scientific Review in 2009

Impact	Score	Descriptor	Strengths/Weaknesses
High Impact	1	Exceptional	Exceptionally strong with essentially no weaknesses
	2	Outstanding	Extremely strong with negligible weaknesses
	3	Excellent	Very strong with only some minor weaknesses
Moderate Impact	4	Very Good	Strong but with numerous minor weaknesses
	5	Good	Strong but with at least one moderate weakness
	6	Satisfactory	Some strengths but also some moderate weaknesses
Low Impact	7	Fair	Some strengths but with at least one major weakness
	8	Marginal	A few strengths and a few major weaknesses
	9	Poor	Very few strengths and numerous major weaknesses

For additional information to assist you in making these determinations, please refer to: http://grants.nih.gov/grants/peer/guidelines_general/Human_Subjects_Protection_and_Inclusion_a5.pdf and http://grants.nih.gov/grants/peer/guidelines_general/Human_Subjects_Worksheet_a5.pdf

Vertebrate Animal Reviewers are asked to evaluate the involvement of live vertebrate animals as part of the scientific assessment according to the following five points: (1) proposed use of the animals, and species, strains, ages, sex, and numbers to be used; (2) justifications for the use of animals and for the appropriateness of the species and numbers proposed; (3) adequacy of veterinary care; (4) procedures for limiting discomfort, distress, pain and injury to that which is unavoidable in the conduct of scientifically sound research including the use of analgesic, anesthetic, and tranquilizing drugs and/or comfortable restraining devices; and (5) methods of euthanasia and reason for selection if not consistent with the AVMA Guidelines on Euthanasia. For additional information to assist you in determining if the Vertebrate Animals section is "Acceptable" or "Unacceptable," please refer to: http://grants.nih.gov/grants/olaw/VASchecklist.pdf.

Biohazards Reviewers will assess whether materials or procedures proposed are potentially hazardous to research personnel and/or the environment, and if needed, determine whether adequate protection is proposed.

SCORING OF THE APPLICATION

In March, 2009, the CSR implemented a new scoring system based on a nine-point scale (**Table 1**). The old scoring scale was based upon a 1 to 5 scale in 0.1 point increments, which allowed a total of 41 "score bins" across the full scoring range. Making 41 discriminations was deemed difficult for reviewers, and, more importantly, scores were becoming compressed at the positive end of the scale. The shift to a nine-point scale in which only whole integers are provided as scores reduces the number of discriminations dramatically. The representative list of descriptors (**Table 1**) indicates that the intent of the scoring system is to broadly categorize applications into thirds. Whereas discriminating between an application scored 1.4 and one scored 1.5 using the old scale may have been difficult, it is felt that using the new scale the discrimination between an application scored as a 3 versus one scored as a 4 should be easier.

After the discussion of your application is completed (see later), each member of the study section will vote an integer score using the 1 – 9 scale. The average of all scores is determined and multiplied by a factor of 10 to obtain the final score ranging between 10 and 90. Your application will be ranked by score, which is the primary, although not only factor used by NIH program when making funding decisions. As this new scoring system has only been recently adopted, it is not possible at this point to assess whether the desired goals of this system are being achieved.

Perhaps the most important change to the scoring system from your perspective as a PI is the feedback obtained by having each of the five criteria assigned a numeric score. Whereas the old scoring system provided one overall score, the new scoring system provides a score for each of the criteria in addition to the overall score. This means that you will know the numeric designation used by the reviewer in ranking *Significance, Investigator(s), Innovation, Approach,* and *Environment.* This type of feedback should make it easier as a PI to determine the areas of the application that were viewed as being weaker or deficient as compared to the old system, in which such information from the reviewers was often disguised within the text of the critique.

THE STUDY SECTION MEETING

STUDY SECTION COMPOSITION AND ATTENDEES

The study section is composed of individuals who play three distinct roles. The Scientific Review Officer (SRO) is the designated federal official responsible for conducting the peer review meeting. The SRO will determine who among the study section members are most appropriate to review your application. Some SROs will make decisions as to who reviews your application after consultation with the Chair of the study section. The Chair of the study section conducts the review meeting with the SRO and serves to direct the discussion of each application. Each application is assigned to three reviewers. At least two of the reviewers will provide written critiques of your application, although generally each of the reviewers provides a written critique. These three individuals lead the discussion of your application during the study section meeting, and it is these individuals who are to serve as advocates for the application. Reviewers of your application may be permanent members serving multi-year terms on the study section, or they may be *ad hoc* members serving for a specific study section meeting. If the SRO determines that no permanent members of the study section have appropriate expertise, s/he will solicit reviews from experts in the field who are not members of the study section but do possess such expertise. These *ad hoc* reviewers will contribute written critiques, but they may participate in the study section meeting by conference call. If an *ad hoc* reviewer has been assigned more than one application to review, they may be invited to attend the study section meeting.

Individuals in addition to permanent and *ad hoc* members of the study section will also attend the meeting. For example, there will be a Grants Management Specialist who will provide administrative support to the SRO. Of most importance to you however, is the presence of NIH extramural staff (i.e., Program Officers or their designees). Make every effort to attend the study section meetings at which applications to which they have been assigned will be reviewed. These individuals may not participate in the discussion of applications, and they do not vote a score. After the review is completed and you have received your score and critiques, you may speak with your Program Officer about the review. If your Program Officer, or designee, was present when your application was reviewed they will have notes about the discussion and will often be able and willing to provide insight into the review, particularly with respect to weaknesses in the application, that may not be totally apparent or clear from the written critique.

MEETING AGENDA

The study section meeting agenda will vary somewhat among SROs, but there are some components that are common to all meetings. The meeting will begin with formalities such as a statement by the SRO of Conflict of Interest (COI) policies and polling the study section members to determine if any COI were inadvertently missed during assignment of applications for review. COI may include, among other things, being from the same institution as the applicant, or being a collaborator/mentor with/of an applicant. The general rule of thumb is that if you have collaborated or published with an individual during the last 5 years, you have a COI that will preclude your participation in the review process for that application. In addition, if you have stated in your cover letter that you have philosophic differences with a member of the study section that may preclude an impartial review of your application, that individual is likely to be identified as having a COI. Any individual who is indentified as having a COI will be excused from the room during the discussion of that particular application and will not vote a score for that application.

The SRO will at some point turn the meeting over to the Chair of the study section and the actual review of the applications will begin. When it is time for your application to be reviewed, the Chair will ask the three reviewers for their preliminary scores. Each reviewer will give an initial score and then the individual designated as the primary reviewer will begin the discussion. The discussion of your application should focus first on the overall hypothesis and an assessment as to the importance of the potential results to the field, and then on the details of the proposed approach.

ASYNCHRONOUS ELECTRONIC DISCUSSION (AED) REVIEW

The AED Review protocol was initiated in 2005. This type of review "meeting" is conducted electronically over a period of (generally) two days. The stated goal of AED Review is to, "provide a new, viable method of scientific peer-review for grant applications submitted to NIH—without the need for concurrent assembly or teleconference." The expected benefits include, "greater flexibility for scheduling peer-review meetings, expanding the potential reviewer base, enhancing the dynamics of discussion at the meeting, simplifying management of conflicts, and reducing costs." Limited AED Review began with the January round of submissions in 2007, and expansion of the AED Review process is still being discussed.

From your perspective as PI, and although an overly-simplified statement, you may think of AED as a fancy threaded message board on which your application is being discussed. There have been several iterations of the software developed for use in the AED review. The general workflow for this type of review is as follows: Your application is submitted and assigned as previously summarized. As with traditional face-to-face study section meetings, reviewers involved in AED Review post by a specified date and time their critiques on a secure Web site accessed *via eRa Commons,* termed *Internet Assisted Review.* Other reviewers involved in the AED Review meeting then have access to read the critiques for a period of several days. On a particular date and time the AED Review Web site becomes available to reviewers, and threaded discussions begin about each application. Comments posted by the reviewers assigned to a specific application are viewable to all study section members involved in the AED Review. Any study section member of the AED Review meeting is able to post comments, ask questions, etc., about any of the applications under review. The thread of comments for each application is maintained such that one can go back and review the entire "discussion" for a particular application.

In addition to the thread of comments, the initial scores of the three reviewers assigned to a particular application are posted. Provision is made for dynamic changes to be made to the scores during the course of the threaded discussion. For example, a reviewer may post a threaded comment indicating that "on the basis of the comment of Reviewer 1, I now have less concerns about the ability of the PI to successfully target brain stem nuclei for microinjection of compounds and am changing my score for *approach* from a 4 to a 3." The new score (3) would be posted in a grid that is visible to all reviewers. The intent of posting "interim" scores is to provide feedback to other reviewers involved in the meeting as to changes in levels of enthusiasm for the application as the threaded discussion progresses. On a specific date and time, the AED Review meeting will end and the threaded discussions cease. There is then a period of several hours when the final scores for each application are entered into the scoring grid. Each member of the study section votes a score electronically for each application. During the days that follow, critiques of the applications may be edited to reflect the threaded discussion.

Although there are benefits to CSR for conducting this type of review meeting, it is not clear there will be benefits to you as a PI. As with face-to-face study section meetings, if the initial assessment/scores of the three reviewers are in very close agreement, there is likely to be little threaded discussion and the scores may not change much from their initial values. However, if there are differences in scores that generate a significant amount of threaded discussion, the inability of AED Review to provide visual and auditory feedback among the reviewers (i.e., assessment of "body language") may well lead to less effective advocacy for a particular application. In addition, whereas much can be verbally communicated in one minute (for example), for most it takes much longer to type a similar amount of information. To what extent threaded discussions lead to less discussion, rather than more, about a particular application has to my knowledge not been determined. Similarly, to my knowledge there has not been a direct comparison of scores voted to specific applications that have been reviewed by AED Review *and* by traditional face-to-face study section meetings to assess differences due to the type of review meeting used. In 2007, CSR surveyed reviewers who had used AED Review during the June and December 2006 review cycles. Of the 232 reviewers who responded, roughly one-third felt the discussions were not as rigorous *or* there were compromises in the review process (http://cms.csr.nih.gov/NR/rdonlyres/5DBA768C-5C75-469B-922D-E96142CB6160/14849/AEDReviewerSurveySummaryDec2006.pdf.) A second survey was planned for the October 2008 review cycle, but the results are not available online as of the publication date for this guide. It must be pointed out that the change to the new nine-point scoring scale and the increase in the use of AED Review are occurring at the same time. There will be a period of re-calibration for reviewers for changes to the scoring system and to the use of AED Review.

THE CRITIQUE ("PINK" SHEET)

Within a week or so (generally) of the study section meeting, the critique of your application will be available on *eRA Commons*. The critique historically was referred to as the "pink" sheet because of the color of the paper on which NIH printed the grant application review (although it has been decades since paper of any color was used by NIH for the critique and for many years the review has been transmitted electronically). As part of the initiative to streamline the review process, in 2009 CSR adopted a critique template that has simplified and standardized the written critique. Written critiques no longer will consist of free-flowing text that often rivaled the grant application itself in terms of length and complexity. Instead, the written review for each scored criteria and for the overall impact/priority of the application is limited to one-quarter page of bulleted statements. Early feedback from reviewers suggests this new template has been generally well-received because it has dramatically reduced the time taken to produce a written critique and it provides incentive to focus the critique only on the big issues of the application.

However, the new critique template does not appear to have been well-received to-date by investigators. The previous review system often resulted in a critique of 5 pages or more, and although the major weaknesses of the application were supposed to be the focus of the critique, there was often a lot of text devoted to issues that in many cases were not central. As an investigator, it was often difficult to extract from these long and complex critiques the most salient information intended by the reviewer. Nevertheless, a lot of feedback was usually provided to the investigator with the old critique format. The new critique template may make it difficult to determine the scope of issues felt by reviewers to be important. As an investigator, you may feel you are getting less information as feedback from the reviewers when reading your critique on this new template. As with other newly-adopted changes to the peer-review process, it will take some time for both reviewers and investigators to adjust to the new critique template.

THE RESUBMISSION

Unfortunately, the vast majority of applications submitted to NIH will fail to achieve a fundable score on the first submission. For many years NIH policy allowed for two revisions to an unfunded application. Recently however, NIH has adopted a policy that applications may be revised only once. That is, an application may be submitted only twice. This reduction in the number of submissions increases the pressure on you as an investigator to make sure every aspect of "grantsmanship" is perfect, insofar as possible. The decision making process as to when an application is "strong enough" to submit now becomes even more critical as there will be minimal margin for error. There are many aspects of the grant application that have been discussed in other chapters of this volume. Suffice it to say that it will now be more important than ever that applications are physically "perfect." Those applications that are "sloppy" (typos, misspelled words, poorly formatted, poor quality graphics for figures, difficult for reviewers to read, etc.) will be at even a greater disadvantage than before. Nevertheless, even applications that are scientifically strong, that pose important questions that can be answered to provide new information that will advance the field, will more often than not require revision.

One of the most important components of the revised application to be re-submitted is the *Introduction to Revised Application* section. The *Introduction to Revised Application* section is to be used to provide a detailed response to concerns raised by the reviewers. Beyond the response to concerns raised, it is also important that the *Introduction* clearly and succinctly articulates the changes that have been made to the application. It is a good idea to begin the *Introduction* by thanking the reviewers for their insightful comments and to point out the positive aspects of the application identified by the reviewers. Since much of the *Introduction* is devoted to addressing the "negative" aspects of the review, it is also important to briefly remind the reviewers of the strengths of the application.

Every effort should be made to make it easy for the reviewers to know exactly what the major changes were and how these changes address the identified weaknesses. After thanking the reviewers for their insightful review, and summarizing the strengths of the application identified by the reviewers, it may be a good idea to provide as an itemized or bulleted list a synopsis of the *major* changes made to the application. One could state, for example:

> "As suggested by the reviewers: (1) Experiment 1 of Specific Aim 1 has been omitted, (2) the number of compounds proposed for testing has been reduced, and (3) an experiment in which X will be antagonized has now been included in Specific Aim 2. In addition, (4) we present *new preliminary data* demonstrating that antagonizing X abolishes Y…"

Such a synopsis will make it much easier for the reviewers to understand the extent to which you have addressed their suggestions.

Although termed *Introduction*, this section is often viewed by investigators as "The Rebuttal." Keep in mind however, that the *Introduction* is all about the reviewers, and not about you. An overly aggressive or argumentative tone on your part will not ingratiate you to the reviewers. Similarly, this is not a debate. Even though you may feel compelled to do so, this is not the time to prove to the reviewer that you actually know more about your proposed project than s/he does. The adage that the "reviewer is always right" is for the most part true when it comes to this section of the application. Some aspects of the review will be inaccurate, and these must be respectfully pointed out. Pointing out information contained in the application that was missed by the reviewer must be done with courtesy and respect. Phrases such as, "I did not clearly articulate that …" are likely to be received in a more positive manner than, "as indicated on page 10 of the application, which the reviewer apparently did not read, …".

The fundamental purpose of the peer-review process is to guide NIH in funding decisions that will result in the best use of tax-payers dollars to the benefit of our physical and mental health. The fundamental purpose of the grant application *critique*, much like that of a manuscript submitted for publication, is to point out weaknesses, which if resolved would make the project stronger, more meaningful, and perhaps increase the probability of success. It is a fact of life, however, that reviewers do not possess expertise in all areas of sleep research and on occasion are not able to/do not give a meaningful review. There will invariably be suggestions as to which experiments should be deleted, or ideas for new/different experiments to be conducted. Some suggestions by the reviewers are just not tenable, whether because of biology, scope of available resources or many other factors. In these instances, you must politely state your reasons and the rationale for not implementing the suggestions of the reviewers. However, in most instances you will agree with the expert advice provided by the reviewers and omit or add experiments, or change the experimental approach/design as suggested. Remember, at this point in the NIH funding process it is definitely not about you, it is all about the reviewers.

There is one aspect of the review to which you should always agree. If there are phrases in the critique such as "overly ambitious," or "this project is unlikely to be completed within the time frame of funding," your application has taken a substantial hit. Often junior faculty or new investigators do not carefully evaluate the *total* work load of the proposed project. When blood or tissue samples are to be used as sources of RNA, DNA or protein which will be assayed by various methods, take the time to calculate the number of *all* the samples that will be collected across the entire study, determine exactly how many assays/plates/reactions, etc., will need to be run and estimate the time it will take to do that. Carefully assess the time it will take to manipulate animals or get human subjects through the entire protocol. The easiest way to assure a poor score upon review is to propose to conduct more work than can be achieved in a reasonable amount of time. Therefore, if comments are made in the critique as to the "overly ambitious" nature of the project, you will *always* agree with the reviewer and reduce the workload by eliminating experiments or manipulations.

The *Introduction* is to be used to address in a point-by-point manner the *major* issues raised by the reviewers. You must also demonstrate where changes have been made and what changes have been made to the body of the text of the application. There are several ways in which changes to the text may be indicated. One may choose to us **boldface type** or *italics font*, but the general principle is that the manner in which changes to the text are indicated should not make it physically difficult to read the application. If extensive changes are made, it may be better to use a vertical notation in the margin, such as available in the Microsoft Word track changes feature. Using a notation in the margin will indicate to the reviewers where

Mark R. Opp, PhD

changes have been without cluttering text with extensive boldface type or italics font. This approach will also allow you to use boldface type and italics fonts for your headings and subheadings, without confusing them with changes to the text. One final note, it is not necessary to indicate every single change you have made to the text. Corrections of inadvertent typos or grammatical errors do not need to be indicated, nor does minor editing to the text. "Reserve" identification of changes that you have made to those of substance that are in response to the critique.

RESOURCES

The CSR Web site contains much useful information about the submission and peer-review process. The major aspects of the submission and peer-review process have been summarized in this chapter, and much of this information was obtained from the CSR Web site. However, there is much more information available, and interested readers, particularly new investigators, are encouraged to make use of these resources during the development and submission of the grant application. The following list of links is arranged more-or-less in a sequence corresponding to the workflow of the submission and peer-review process.

Center for Scientific Review (CSR) home:
http://cms.csr.nih.gov/

Welcome to CSR:
http://cms.csr.nih.gov/AboutCSR/Welcome+to+CSR/

Submission and assignment process:
http://cms.csr.nih.gov/ResourcesforApplicants/Submission+And+Assignment+Process.htm

What happens to your application:
http://cms.csr.nih.gov/AboutCSR/OverviewofPeerReviewProcess.htm

Insider's guide to peer review for applicants:
http://cms.csr.nih.gov/nr/rdonlyres/60b2d32e-ae00-4358-8c51-2e11cc46eac8/15100/insiderguideapplicantsfinal.pdf

Mock study section video:
http://cms.csr.nih.gov/ResourcesforApplicants/InsidetheNIHGrantReviewProcessVideo.htm

The "peer review process":
http://cms.csr.nih.gov/AboutCSR/OverviewofPeerReviewProcess.htm

Asynchronous Electronic Discussion Review:
http://cms.csr.nih.gov/AboutCSR/CSRInitiativesNew/RecruitingtheBestReviewers/AEDReview.htm

Quick links: answers for applicants:
http://cms.csr.nih.gov/ResourcesforApplicants/QuickLinks-AnswersforApplicants.htm

Chapter X

Implementing the Grant Proposal

Clete A. Kushida, MD, PhD

Study Organization and Timeline

The organization and reporting structure for a study needs to be well-designed and carefully planned. For large clinical trials, it is important to have Coordinating Centers, such as a Data Coordinating Center (DCC) and a Clinical Coordinating Center (CCC), as well as committees and teams that manage specific aspects of the study. As an example, the study organization for the National Heart, Lung, and Blood Institute (NHLBI)-sponsored Apnea Positive Pressure Long-term Efficacy Study (APPLES) is shown in **Figure 1** (Kushida et al., 2006).

Figure 1

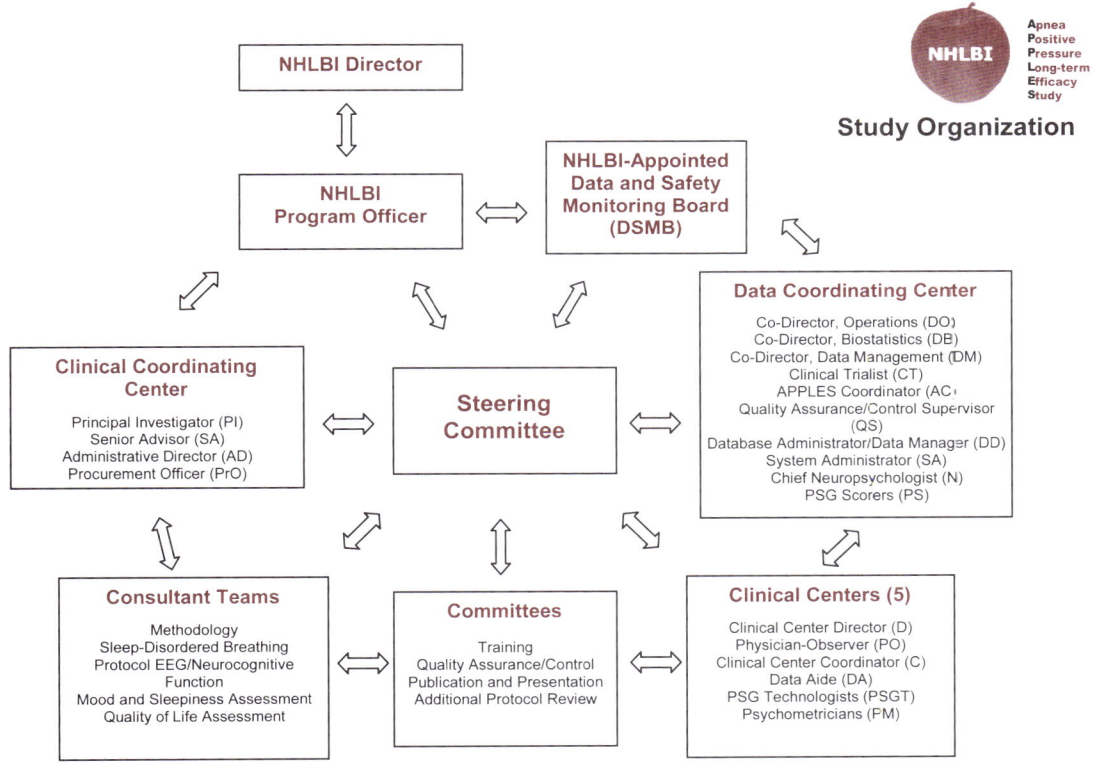

It is also important to meticulously plan out the timeline of the study, and to factor in a reasonable planning phase for the development of the protocol and manual operations, to standardize the data collection procedures, and to train the study's personnel. Similarly, it is important to add sufficient time at the end of the study for data analysis, preparation of manuscripts and presentation, and to closeout the sites. The study timeline for APPLES is shown in **Figure 2**.

Figure 2

Study Organization

	9/1/02	9/1/03	9/1/04	9/1/05	9/1/06	8/1/07	7/31/08
Year	1	2	3	4	5	6	
Month	1-------12	13-------24	25-------36	37-------48	49-------59	60-------71	
Phase I							
Planning & Protocol	▮						
Phase II							
Subject Recruitment		▮	▮	▮	▮	▮	
Follow up Data Collection		▮	▮	▮	▮	▮	
Phase III							
Data Analysis					▮	▮	
Report Preparation					▮	▮	
Study Closeout						▮	

PROTOCOL AND MANUAL OF OPERATIONS DEVELOPMENT

A detailed protocol and manual of operations (see Operations Core, pg 125) ensure success of the study. The initial grant application can be used as a template for the ensuing protocol and manual of operations. Adequate time should be allowed for construction of these documents since they will serve as the blueprints for the conduct of the study. Although the functions may overlap, the protocol serves as a detailed description of the study including all methods and procedures of the study, whereas the manual of operations is typically an even more detailed handbook-type reference that is used by the personnel in the study to conduct all aspects of the study.

STUDY OVERSIGHT

STEERING COMMITTEE

The Steering Committee is in charge of the overall direction of the study, and has close communication with the CCC and DCC. The size of a Steering Committee is typically dependent on the size of the study. In general, it can include the Principal Investigator, Project Director, key CCC and DCC personnel, Biostatistician(s), Site Directors, Site Coordinators, and the NIH Program Officer. The inclusion of other key personnel can be included as considered necessary by the study's Executive Committee (e.g., Principal Investigator, Project Director, key personnel). The Executive Committee should also decide which members of the Steering Committee should have voting privileges. Generally, any members that have conflicts-of-interest (e.g., industry consultants) and/or have less key roles in the study do not necessarily need to be voting members. Conference calls for this committee are usually scheduled on at least a monthly basis, and an annual face-to-face meeting should be arranged.

NIH PROGRAM OFFICER

The NIH Program Officer is responsible for the oversight of the conduct of the study. The NIH Program Officer works with the Data and Safety Monitoring Board to ensure that quality assurance functions are adequately performed by the Data Coordinating Center. The NIH Program Officer may monitor progress by regular communication with the Principal Investigator and the Data and Safety Monitoring Board. Since continuation of an award is conditional upon satisfactory progress, the NIH Program Officer should be periodically updated by the Data Coordinating Center with respect to the completion of important steps, such as recruitment milestones and accrual goals for women and minority subjects. It is also important to have the NIH Program Officer of the study participate in conference calls and meetings of the Steering Committee, since this NIH representative can provide information that can be helpful to the Steering Committee (e.g., policy decisions, new funding opportunities).

DATA AND SAFETY MONITORING BOARD (DSMB)

The external Data and Safety Monitoring Board (DSMB) should be established in all clinical trials and its members appointed in consultation with the NIH. The board members will report directly to the NIH and will not be associated with any of the institutions participating in this study. The roles of this NIH-appointed board are to ensure the safety of the subjects and the scientific integrity of the study. The roles of the board typically include: (a) serving as an independent advisory group providing guidance on subject safety issues; (b) supervising the overall safety of the study and recommending study termination due to unacceptable adverse effects; (c) monitoring the quality control activities of the DCC; (d) assessing the performance of the individual sites; and (e) recommending possible modifications in the clinical trial protocol.

A DSMB is an important component of clinical trials, and DSMB selection and conference calls/meetings should be factored into the study timeline. It is similarly important to add in the costs of these conference calls/meetings and honoraria for DSMB members into your budget. Selection of the DSMB membership is by the NIH Program Officer; however, NIH will often request that the study investigators propose a list of scientists who are knowledgeable about the study's area of interest and who would be good candidates for the DSMB. The charges of DSMBs are typically to monitor the progress of the study and to ensure the safety of the participants. Included within the scope of their monitoring of the study is their decision to halt the study early, typically by a priori "stopping rules," if the DSMB members believe that further continuation of study will be futile (i.e., conclusion of the study will not result in a definite answer to the primary outcome), danger to the participants (e.g., one of the treatment arms poses a significant health risk to the participants), or significant differences in the primary outcome between the arms (i.e., early efficacy is observed making additional participants unwarranted). The DSMB has the opportunity to review the unblinded data and thus is in a good position to assess if there is an imbalance in the adverse events of the arms. For example, if participants in one of the arms have a significantly greater mortality than the participants in the other arm, the DSMB might consider early termination of the study. DSMBs often have considerable latitude in their control of the study, since almost any aspect of a study influences study efficacy and participant safety; the DSMB may even recommend a change in a protocol that has already passed through peer review as part of the grant application process and has been approved by the institutional review board. It is the responsibility of the study personnel to schedule and arrange all DSMB conference calls and meetings, and to prepare the agendas and reports.

CLINICAL COORDINATING CENTER (CCC)

For large-scale clinical trials, a Clinical Coordinating Center (CCC) can be important. The primary function of a CCC is to serve as the administrative and communications hub for the study. Typical responsibilities are: (a) organizing conference calls, meetings, training sessions, and site visits; (b) ensuring subject safety and compliance with institutional review boards; (c) developing mechanisms to ensure a smooth transfer of data between the sites and the DCC; (d) assisting in the procurement of equivalent forms, tests, and equipment to be used by the sites; (e) ensuring compliance with deadlines; (f) ensuring compliance with protocols and procedures (e.g., subject recruitment, randomization); and (g) monitoring federal regulatory compliance, fiscal and personnel management, and development of conflict-of-interest policies. Most importantly, the CCC will work with the key investigators to assume the leadership role in maintaining the scientific integrity, cooperation, and morale among the sites.

The CCC serves a vital role as the communications hub for the study, maintaining easy access between sites and investigators via multiple communication methods, including voice, fax, email, and the study's Web site. The CCC typically schedules, organizes, and prepares the agendas and minutes for the conference calls and meetings.

The Principal Investigator should visit each site at least once a year with the following goals in mind: (a) to monitor each Clinical Center's organization and procedures; (b) to promote comparability and standardization of procedures; (c) to gain understanding of special problems facing each Clinical Center (CC); (d) to establish rapport with the CC staff; and (e) to promote and maintain enthusiasm for the study. The Principal Investigator should be especially attuned to evaluate protocol violations, testing, forms and questionnaire completion and filing, data entry and error correction, randomization procedures, organization of staff and laboratory space, morale, enthusiasm of the staff and CC Director, rapport with subjects, professional appearance of the laboratory, adequacy and cleanliness of space, logistics of subject involvement, recruitment and scheduling efficacy, laboratory parking and access for subjects, and subject wait times. A site visit report should be compiled by the Principal Investigator (after verification by the NIH Project/Program Officer by e-mail or fax), and then sent to the CC Director within a month following the site visit.

PERSONNEL TRAINING

The time needed to adequately train personnel is frequently underestimated in the planning of a study. It becomes even more important in large-scale clinical trials that involve multiple sites, since it is important that these sites are standardized to the protocol and manual or operations. The DCC typically trains personnel at the sites on the methods and procedures for data acquisition. This includes the following:
- Screening, subject enrollment, and randomization procedures
- Standardization of the testing and other procedures
- Administration of the testing and procedures

The initial start-up period (typically three to six months) is devoted to personnel training and setup, and the CC Directors should meet one to two times with DCC personnel for extensive education and training on the study protocol. Each CC Director can be accompanied by the CC Coordinator. These training sessions will include methodology regarding standardized testing and other procedures, subject coding, randomization and blinding, subject interviews and testing, data collection and management, and transfer of data to the DCC. A written examination, based solely on the manual of operations, can be considered; it could be administered to all CC Coordinators within one month after the initial centralized training session. Any CC Coordinator with a score less than a standardized cutoff score (e.g., 95 percent) should be administered a repeat examination.

In addition to this initial training the CC Directors should plan to travel one to two times a year for the four years of data acquisition for review of the study protocol and procedures. DCC personnel should also plan to visit each site once a year to assist the sites with the study protocol and procedures. These individuals should visit each site with the following items in mind: (a) review of randomization procedures; (b) review of database inventory and updates, and procedure documentation; (c) data and program file backup procedures; (d) data analysis and quality assurance program procedures; (e) organizational structure; and (f) quality assurance procedures, including an audit of study records, and comparison of original documents with database files.

During the course of a long-term study, staff turnover will be inevitable. To minimize turnover, sites should be encouraged to hire staff personnel who are likely to remain for the long term and to request immediate notice when staff personnel leave the study. Whenever possible, a newly-hired CC Coordinator should be trained and supervised on-site by either the departing CC Coordinator or the CC Director to ensure a smooth transition without significant interruption of data collection.

INFORMED CONSENT

MULTICENTER CONSIDERATIONS

Each Clinical Center should thoroughly discuss the study (including potential risks and other treatment options) with a potential subject. If the subject meets study criteria for inclusion and decides to participate in the study, informed consent should be obtained. The subjects should then be given the informed consent forms from each site's institutional review board for review and signature. The DCC should monitor that each enrolled subject has a signed consent form on file at the respective site; however, due to confidentiality issues, the DCC should not request a copy of the consent form for each subject.

GENETIC TESTING

If the protocol requires genetic testing on blood samples, the DCC should coordinate the language of the informed consent to ensure each subject's rights are protected particularly with respect to the specific genetic testing and/or screening for particular diseases. The DCC and each Clinical Center should monitor that the timing of the collection and destruction of the blood samples do not exceed the limits stated in the informed consent, and that the blood samples are not used for other genetic testing or additional uses not covered within the scope of the informed consent.

PARTICIPANT RECRUITMENT AND RETENTION

Participant recruitment and retention are paramount to the success of the study. Selection of Clinical Centers that have a good track record for meeting recruitment and retention goals is key, and sites should be carefully selected to balance and adequately ensure gender and minority representation. The grant application and subsequent protocol should specify in detail the participant recruitment timeline and milestones. The recruitment and retention of participants should also be a critical part of any report to the DSMB, and the Steering Committee should also review these data on a frequent basis.

Clete A. Kushida, MD, PhD

Recruitment may be slow due to fluctuations in outpatient populations, poor organization, or inadequate recruitment at specific sites. To minimize this problem, the DCC should report the rates and reasons for ineligibility, overall and stratified by specific site, on a frequent (e.g., monthly) basis. In the event of poor subject recruitment at a specific Clinical Center, a site visit by DCC personnel may be required. Procedures to specifically increase participant recruitment and retention should also be described in the grant application and protocol, and these procedures should be implemented without delay. Gender and minority representation should also be closely monitored, and adequate plans to compensate for lagging recruitment or retention should be documented.

DATA MANAGEMENT

QUALITY ASSURANCE AND CONTROL

As part of the DCC, it is a good idea to hire a Quality Assurance Supervisor, who has experience with quality control methodology and procedures. This person will be responsible for ensuring that the data collection and analysis procedures for all sites are uniform and of the highest quality. This responsibility is also shared with the Principal Investigator and Project Director, and, at each site, the CC Director and CC Coordinator supervise quality control. The CC Coordinator will also typically serve as a member of the Quality Control Committee. Staff at the DCC will independently review the data for consistency and compliance using quality control and assurance protocols developed by the center. The examination of the data will include identification of possible missing, inconsistent, and outlying data specifically in the areas of subject enrollment and data quality.

In APPLES, all of the polysomnograms and maintenance of wakefulness tests were blindly scored by the DCC polysomnographic technologist, and 5 percent of these tests were randomly and blindly scored by the DCC data technologist. If the scored data (e.g., respiratory disturbance indices [RDI], sleep stage percentages) from the polysomnographic technologist and the data technologist differ by more than 5 percent, the two technologists, the Quality Assurance Supervisor, and the DCC Co-Director of Operations reviewed the data and the recordings together. The aims of these meetings were to discuss the discrepancies in scoring, to reach a consensus regarding the discrepant data, and to implement corrections in scoring practices. If discrepancies between the data dually-scored by the polysomnographic and data technologists continued, further correction actions were planned such as requiring review sessions on scoring and increasing the dual scoring requirement to 10 percent of all tests. However, for the scoring of sleep studies, or any important outcomes, it is important to hire only highly experienced registered personnel with many years of scoring and managing the types of outcomes in the study.

Standardization of data input is important, and methods such as double-data entry into a secure Web site maintained by the DCC can serve to minimize errors. There is a minimum of important data which typically need to be manually entered at the individual CCs (e.g., subject demographic information); however, these data can be verified by having the individual CCs mail in copies of their original data sheets to the DCC. For other data that the individual sites manually enter into the Web site, the DCC typically should randomly review a portion (e.g., 10 percent) of the original data. If this monitoring technique indicates a systematic problem for a particular site, the DCC may review 100 percent of the original data. In addition, DCC personnel should visit each site twice a year; one of the reasons for these visits is data review. The DCC should have its own procedures for internal quality control, which include periodic assessment of data collection and flow, data processing and analysis time, and procedures to minimize data errors.

INTERIM ANALYSES

The DCC, DSMB, and NIH, may collaboratively decide to examine the efficacy and safety data of the study two to three times prior to the conclusion of the study. Typically, these interim analyses are temporally connected to subject participation in the study (e.g., 50 percent interim analysis when 50 percent of the subjects have completed the study). The Principal Investigator and key personnel are in charge of reviewing these data with the DSMB, and it is the DSMB charge to determine whether the study can continue following review of these data. The key factors in the decision by the DSMB are if the subjects' safety is not at risk and if the study's principal aims have already been achieved warranting early termination of the study (see Data and Safety Monitoring Board, pg 121). The study personnel must be careful as to who can present the unblinded vs. blinded data to the DSMB lest a study team member becomes inadvertently unblinded.

DATA SHARING AND COLLABORATION

In a large and high-profile study, it is not unusual to receive requests for sharing of the study's data or collaboration on an additional project. It is helpful for committees comprised of study personnel (i.e., Publication and Presentation Committee, Additional Protocol Review Committee, Steering Committee) to make decisions regarding these requests. Formal request forms and rules developed by these committees can make this process more efficient and consistent.

DATA COORDINATING CENTER ROLES AND RESPONSIBILITIES

The Data Coordinating Center (DCC) usually exists as an independent unit from the study, and functions as an "umbrella" support organization providing the necessary skills and expertise for a successful multicenter study. From a global perspective, the DCC works to provide a seamless integration of data collection and analysis efforts across the entire project. The DCC typically maintains rapport and communication with the: (a) NIH Program Officer; (b) NIH-Appointed Data and Safety Monitoring Board; (c) Committees (e.g., Steering, Training, Quality Control, and Publication); (d) Clinical Coordinating Center (CCC), or the administrative and communication core of the study; (e) Consultant Teams; and (f) Individual Sites (Clinical Centers). Rapid and effective communication between the DCC, CCC, and Clinical Centers (CCs) is essential and should be encouraged, with priority given to questions from CC Directors and CC Coordinators. In conjunction with the CCC, the DCC takes the leadership role in the maintenance of both the morale and scientific integrity of the study (Meinert, 1986).

It is often helpful to conceptually or practically divide the DCC into three core groups. While each core will have a distinct role they actively interact to provide a cohesive support structure for the project. The personnel staffing the cores (Operations, Biostatistics, Data Management) should meet on a regular basis to discuss the progress of the study and to address any pending issues. The objectives of the three cores are described below:

Operations Core

1. *Coordinate the setup of equipment and communication links at the DCC, CCC, and all Clinical Centers, including the installation of the data acquisition systems required for transmission of the data from the Clinical Centers to the DCC.* Each Clinical Center can communicate with the DCC and CCC via Internet connections. Computers, servers, and backup servers should provide a presence on the Internet with sufficient bandwidth to allow rapid, password-protected data transfer with the remote Clinical Centers. DCC personnel should travel to each CC to assist in the setup of the equipment and communication links.

Clete A. Kushida, MD, PhD

2. *Coordinate all data collection at the Clinical Centers and data transmission to the DCC.* The DCC should work closely with the CC Coordinators at each site to ensure efficient and timely data collection. The Operations Core should monitor transmission of data from the Clinical Centers to the DCC to ensure that the data is uniform and readable.

3. *Serve as a central scoring facility for the test data.* One of the primary roles of the DCC can be to serve as a central scoring facility, by receiving data collected from the testing. In the case of sleep-related studies, the DCC can receive polysomnographic (PSG) data collected using a standardized protocol, and translate it into a standard file format, which polysomnographic technologists at the DCC can then manually and blindly score. In any case, it is important for the DCC to use a system that successfully allows data acquired by diverse equipment from different sites to be converted, transmitted, and read in a common format.

4. *Train and monitor personnel at the sites on the methods and procedures for data acquisition* (see Personnel Training, pg 122)

5. *Distribute training materials and documentation (including the manual of operations) through the project Web site.* The DCC and the individual sites should use a manual of operations for data management; this complete manual should be distributed to all study personnel, and should include material such as: (a) schedules of subject enrollment, testing, and follow-up visits, key events for the subjects, and testing for the subjects; (b) informed consent; (c) assignment of subject code; (d) protocols for the initial evaluation, training sessions, testing, randomization and blinding, and follow-up visits; (e) adherence and safety issues; (f) DCC reporting procedures; (g) technical considerations regarding testing and equipment; and (h) forms and questionnaires. Throughout the study, the manual of operations should also be available on the study's Web site as an online reference.

6. *Independently review all data for consistency and adherence using quality control and assurance protocols developed by the Biostatistics Core.* The DCC Quality Assurance (QA) Supervisor should report directly to the Director of the Operations Core and should work closely with the Biostatistics and Data Management Cores in the implementation of a DCC QA program.

Biostatistics Core

1. *Ensure biostatistical consultation and support are readily available to all investigators.* The Biostatistics Core plays a crucial role by being involved in all the components of scientific research – from the time an idea comes to mind through the design, execution, analysis and reporting of the results. The Biostatistics Core should have input in the conception of the study design, especially with respect to sample-size calculations and the proposed statistical methods.

2. *Provide statistical analytic support and assist the investigators with the statistical analysis and preparation of the data for publication.*

3. *Work closely with the Data Management Core to provide and maintain a database of results.* Frequent interaction with the Data Management Core ensures that the organizational structure of the database will allow efficient access for the Biostatistics Core as well as all other qualified researchers.

4. *Conduct special statistical studies to support the research objectives, ensure that the statistical methods used by investigators are state-of-the-art, and to develop new statistical methods as needed.* In the course of any study, new research questions will arise. The Biostatistics Core should work with investigators to ensure that the most appropriate statistical techniques are adhered to for these analyses. Even in the best run studies, missing data occur, and the DCC should research methods of dealing with missing data.

5. *Monitor data quality by assisting the Data Management Core and Operations Core in implementing quality assurance programs.* The Biostatistics Core should work with the Quality Assurance Supervisor, Quality Control Committee, and the other two Cores to design, develop, and implement appropriate quality assurance studies and reporting procedures (see Quality Assurance and Control, pg 124).

6. *Provide randomization of subjects and monitor subject recruitment.* The Biostatistics Core should direct the randomization procedure of subjects at each site, and should ensure that the study's arms are balanced with respect to the pre-selected randomization factors (e.g., gender, race/ethnic representation). The DCC should also monitor the study recruitment at each site over the course of the trial.

7. *Work with the Publication and Presentation Committee to monitor manuscript preparation.* The Biostatistics Core should work with the Publication and Presentation Committee in manuscript preparation. Specifically, the Biostatistics Core will assist the authors in the statistical analyses of the data.

Data Management Core

1. *Serve as the primary repository for all data by developing and maintaining a centralized database, work with the DCC Programmer/Database Manager in developing the database file structure and dictionary (i.e., variable definitions), and work with the Operations Core to develop the necessary techniques for integrating the wide variety of data received from the Clinical Centers into the project database.* The DCC should be the primary repository for all data collected by the Clinical Centers. The data should be transferred to the DCC via a secure method, such as through a password-protected website. The DCC should develop a database that can effectively collect and store the data from the individual sites. The Quality Assurance Supervisor should review the data at regular intervals.

2. *Develop the procedures necessary to provide the Biostatistics Core and the Clinical Centers access to the data in a format suitable for analysis.* Once the database has been constructed, the Data Management Core should select the core analytic software. This analytic data set should then be available for the DCC and Clinical Center to access.

3. *Work with the Quality Assurance Supervisor, Quality Control Committee, and the Operations and Biostatistics Cores in implementing appropriate quality assurance procedures.*

4. *Provide the Operations Core routine and timely reports on subject recruitment and retention by monitoring data input.* Working closely with the Operations Core to develop effective data entry and importation routines and the Biostatistics Core, Quality Control Committee, and Quality Assurance Supervisor to develop appropriate QA tools, the DCC should be able to closely monitor both subject recruitment and retention as well as frequency of missing data.

Data collected at the Clinical Centers and then transferred to the DCC can typically be categorized as follows:

Primary Data Input. In many instances raw data are transferred from the subject to a computer directly, either by electrodes attached to the subject connected to the computer or by the subject performing a task on the computer. The resultant data files can be transferred to the DCC via the Internet. For sleep-related studies, this applies to sleep stage and respiratory data collected during the polysomnograms, wake and sleep data from the maintenance of wakefulness tests, and test score data from computer-based testing.

Data Retrieval from Peripheral Recording Devices. Data are recorded and stored in peripheral devices; these data are transferred to a computer through a special interface device. The data files can be then transferred to the DCC via the Internet.

Clete A. Kushida, MD, PhD

Forms and Questionnaires. A secure, password-protected Web site can provide a central repository for all documents produced by the DCC. This includes the manual of operations, data collection instruments, interview forms, questionnaires, protocols, data files, and summary sheets for tests not available in computerized versions.

All data collected by the sites should be forwarded to the DCC. For electronic transfer of data to the DCC, a secure, password-protected Web site can be an efficient method for making data and critical study information instantly accessible to all researchers involved with the study. For subject confidentiality, once a subject has been randomized, all subject identifiers on data transmitted via the Internet should be removed. Only assigned, unique subject identification codes should be used to identify the subjects. All data should also be encrypted prior to electronic transmission, in compliance with the Health Insurance Portability and Accountability Act (HIPAA).

Password protection and file locking should be implemented to protect the security and confidentiality of subject databases in both DCC and CC workstations. Multi-level security access should ensure that only appropriate personnel will have the authority to review the subject data, which should be stored in a separate location on a server. Basic identifying information from the records should be automatically and simultaneously added to a separate administrative database, so that the DCC can track and report study progress.

Data can be automatically or manually entered into computerized databases at the DCC. Processing of data at the DCC can be through an integrated data management system which includes subject identification, registration, tracking, storage, cleaning, and inspection of subject data. The input to the database from the Clinical Centers can be primarily via the Internet as described above. An up-to-date subject roster should be maintained on the DCC server as an Internet-enabled transaction database server. This roster can serve as the primary index for subject data, by linking the assigned, unique subject identification codes with the imported data from the Clinical Centers. Tracking of subject data can be performed using this centralized database; client programs at the Clinical Centers can access this database to perform roster-related functions and to enter data. Other data can arrive at the DCC asynchronously from the Clinical Centers. These include data such as from registration and randomization, subject examinations, and testing. The DCC should first check any incoming computer or hardcopy files for correct formatting, missing data, valid ranges, and internal consistency. The DCC should remove duplicate or non-study data, after checking with the CC Coordinator at the site of data origin. Apparently clean and complete records should then be flagged as such and merged with the accumulating subject results database. Error reports that identify incorrect or missing data should be sent from the DCC to the CC Coordinators. The records containing the defective data should be kept in a separate database at the DCC, until correct results are returned to the DCC, at which time the DCC can add these results to the database. The DCC should perform these inspection procedures on the data from the Clinical Centers on a daily basis, in order to identify and correct defective or missing imported data in a timely manner.

EFFICACY ANALYSES OF PRIMARY AND SECONDARY OUTCOMES

The DCC should assist with the statistical analysis and preparation of the data for publication. In the final year of the study, the DCC should assist the key investigators in summarizing the data and performing statistical analyses on the data. The initial statistical analysis typically consists of baseline characteristics of study subjects, presented as descriptive statistics (i.e., means, standard deviations, 95 percent confidence intervals). The Biostatistics Core of the DCC should expend considerable time and effort in the development of a statistical analysis plan for the primary and secondary outcomes. Selection of an expert panel for outside consultation in the development of an analysis plan can sometimes be helpful in the analysis of tests and measures that the Steering Committee lacks familiarity. The Steering Committee and outside consultants can help in deciding which exploratory outcomes to analyze following the analysis of the primary and secondary outcomes.

PARTICIPANT SAFETY

ADVERSE EVENT MONITORING AND REPORTING
A thorough plan for adverse event monitoring and reporting should be formulated well in advance of the initiation of the study. The protocol and manual of operations for the study should indicate the management of adverse events (AEs), including the reporting structure and timelines for notifying the institutional review boards (IRBs) at the sites and the DSMB for serious AEs (SAEs). Methods and procedures for managing expected AEs should be discussed and included in the protocol and manual of operations in advance of the study. The study personnel should prepare a listing of AEs to the DSMB at regular intervals.

PARTICIPANT EDUCATION TO MITIGATE RISKS
The DCC should carefully assess the potential risks to the subjects. The subjects should be informed in detail of the risks proposed in this study and that the investigators will take all precautions necessary to ensure participant safety. The subjects should be notified, if applicable, that they have the opportunity to benefit from the information gathered. If applicable, the study results should be reviewed with the subjects, and if they request so, the information should be forwarded to their physicians. The subjects should also be informed of the risks that might occur if they are randomized to a placebo or sham arm, and what can be done to minimize these risks. For example, if there is a risk of motor-vehicle or work-related accidents as a result of drowsiness or falling asleep, the subjects could be advised to limit their driving to short distances, letting others drive them, or driving with alert passengers. The subjects should be instructed that they will be able to start conventional treatment (if applicable) after the study concludes, that alternative treatments for their condition or disease are available, and that the subjects have the option of exiting from the study and exploring these other treatments. The subjects should be informed that their decision whether or not to participate will not prejudice them or their medical care. The subjects should be further informed that if they decide to participate, they are free to withdraw their consent and to discontinue participation at any time without prejudice to them or effect on their medical care. The subjects should be informed of any compensation or benefits that they will receive for completion of their participation in the study. In addition, they should be informed if any costs associated with the study will be covered by the study, as well as the costs for which the subjects or their insurance companies will be responsible. Lastly, the subjects should be advised that they may be withdrawn from the study for failure to follow instructions, if the investigators decide that continuation could be harmful to the subject, if the subject requires treatment not allowed in the study, if the study is cancelled, or for other administrative reasons.

MEDICAL ALERTS
There are expected and unexpected medical issues that occur during the course of any study. It is important to have good screening procedures to exclude subjects with serious medical or psychiatric conditions from the study. In addition, it is prudent to have a mechanism involving criteria for medical issues or conditions

Clete A. Kushida, MD, PhD

and safety officers (see Safety Officers, below), who can be notified should a medical issue arise in one of the subjects. For example, the study might have specific blood pressure criteria that warrant notification of the subject's primary care physician at their next regularly scheduled visit or an immediate visit to the emergency room.

SAFETY OFFICERS

An independent safety officer or physician-observer should be considered where subjects may be at significant safety risk during the course of the study. This physician-observer is blinded to the subject's treatment assignment, and can contact the subject by telephone and/or meet with each subject at scheduled visits during the course of the subject's participation in the study to assess issues. During the course of each contact with the subject, the physician-observer can explore any safety issues or adverse events. Safety issues can include: (a) hazardous operation of a motor vehicle ("near misses" or drowsiness while driving), or (b) the development of any medical or psychiatric condition that could potentially worsen with the untreated disease under study, increase the impact of the subject's disease on his or her health, or exacerbate the subject's disease-associated risk of injury or death. Adverse events can range from easily solvable problems to the more serious problem of disease-related injuries. These safety issues and adverse events need to be documented in detail. The DCC should review these data on a daily basis; any serious safety concerns should be discussed with the physician-observer. If the physician-observer determines the subject is at risk, the assigned treatment can be deemed a "failure" for purposes of analysis of outcome, and a change in treatment should be offered following a discussion of treatment options. However, since most controlled trials are intention-to-treat, the study personnel should continue to monitor the subject and he or she should be encouraged to return for post-treatment testing or visits. All safety data should be summarized by the study personnel and forwarded to the DSMB on a frequent basis.

PERFORMANCE ASSESSMENT AND ADHERENCE TO PROTOCOL AND TIMELINES

The DCC is responsible for assessing the performance of the study personnel and ensuring that there is adherence of the personnel to the protocol and timelines. In particular, some sites may fail to adhere to various parts of the study protocol. To minimize the occurrence of these violations, the DCC should closely monitor each site for recruitment, subject retention and data quality through routine, systematic and timely execution of a quality assurance program developed by the DCC. The program should specify the criteria for a protocol violation and deviation, and should indicate the steps to correct the violation or deviation. The DCC Quality Assurance Supervisor or the Principal Investigator should notify the CC Coordinator to immediately correct a problem situation. Any Clinical Center that persistently fails to comply with the protocol should be considered for replacement. The DCC should include in its regular reports to the DSMB a section on performance assessment that includes a report of protocol violations and deviations.

ANCILLARY STUDIES

The most important point is that ancillary studies should not interfere with the main study; this means that ancillary studies should avoid using resources, equipment, supplies and personnel designated for the main study. It is good practice to have these studies carefully monitored by an Additional Protocol Review committee of the core team to ensure that no significant overlap exists; the DSMB should also be aware of these studies. It is also important to have the ancillary team submit their study protocol and consent through their local institutional review board (IRB), and, in some cases submit these materials through the parent study's IRB.

PUBLICATIONS AND PRESENTATIONS

For larger studies, it may be beneficial to have a Publication and Presentation (P&P) Committee. This committee (typically selected from the pool of Clinical Center Directors and Consultants) is responsible for the rapid and accurate dissemination of study results by internal review of all publications originating from the study. This committee usually solicits ideas and proposals for publication topics and prioritizes them, supervises the selection of the writing groups, monitors the manuscripts' progress, and reviews the manuscripts. Arranging the conference calls and distribution of the agendas, minutes, and policies is typically the shared responsibility of this committee and the Clinical Coordinating Center. In addition, this committee reviews the content of any oral presentation of the data resulting from the study.

STUDY CLOSEOUT

DATA CLEANUP AND VERIFICATION

The DCC should ensure that it has copies of all key data from each Clinical Center and that there is a process in place to verify that these data are the same as those data at the Clinical Center. As the study closeout commences, it is critical to ensure that there is an adequate backup plan for the data collected during the study.

DATA STORAGE

The DCC serves as the primary repository for all collected data; it is important for the DCC to ensure that the Clinical Centers adequately store the important subject files and data and that enough funds are allocated for storage of these documents. The sites should be responsible for safely storing the data of their subjects, since it is often not practical for the sites to ship these documents to the DCC. The CC workstations should be backed-up weekly with the data media stored off-site. The DCC server should be backed-up daily to ensure no loss of data. Daily backup tapes should be retained for a minimum of two weeks, the last tape for each week should be retained for at least three months. A monthly backup tape should also be made on the last day of each month, and kept for at least one year. All tapes should be stored off-site in a locked and secure facility. The DCC should inform the sites as to when they can destroy unnecessary documents as per NIH guidelines.

DISSEMINATION OF RESULTS AND DATA REPORTING GUIDELINES

The DCC and the Publication and Presentation Committee should be aware of the NIH timeline for dissemination of the principal findings of the study and the reporting of the data. The DCC should also ensure that it is compliant with the data sharing policies of the NIH, and that a mechanism (e.g., website) is in place to allow the data obtained by the study to be seen and used by outside investigators.

REFERENCES

1. Kushida CA, Nichols DA, Quan SF, Goodwin JL, White DP, Gottlieb DJ, Walsh JK, Schweitzer PK, Guilleminault C, Simon RD, Leary EB, Hyde PR, Holmes TH, Bloch DA, Green S, McEvoy LK, Gevins A, Dement WC. The Apnea Positive Pressure Long-term Efficacy Study (APPLES): Rationale, design, methods, and procedures. J Clin Sleep Med 2006;2:288-300.

2. Meinert C. Clinical Trials: Design, Conduct and Analysis. New York, Oxford University Press, 1986.

Clete A. Kushida, MD, PhD

A

AASM, 11, 13
ability, 16, 24, 29, 38, 40, 44, 49, 59, 74, 77, 88, 89,
    91, 115
ACVB, 75
additional protocol review committee, 125, 130
adverse event, 47, 50, 121, 129, 130
adverse event monitoring, 129
adverse event reporting, 129
advisor, 15, 22, 32, 34, 119
AE, 129
American Academy of Sleep Medicine, 11, 13, 80
analytic data set, 127
ancillary studies, 130
anesthesia, 63, 64, 73, 76
animal models, 63-8, 70, 71, 80, 83
animal species, 64-6, 69, 70, 72, 73
antisense, 66, 68, 69, 81
APLAC, 63
Apnea Positive Pressure Long-term Efficacy Study
    (APPLES), 11, 119, 124, 131
Asynchronous Electronic Discussion (AED) Review,
    114, 115, 131
authority, 23, 75, 128
AVMA, 64, 73, 79, 80, 82, 112
awards, 15-9, 28, 42, 95

B

bibliophile, 24
biographical sketch, 28, 35
biosafety, 72
biostatistical consultation, 126
biostatistician, 101, 120
biostatistics core, 126-8
blinding, 53-7, 123, 126
budget, 38, 72, 95

C

career, 11, 13, 15-9, 23-6, 30, 37
career development, 15-9, 23, 25, 26, 30, 31, 34
career development activities, 23, 24
cat, 65, 71
Center for Scientific Review, 85, 86, 107, 112, 118
central scoring facility, 126
citation, 28, 35
clinical center (CC), 119, 122-8, 130, 131
coordinator, 119
director, 119, 131
clinical coordinating center (CCC), 119, 120, 122,
    125
coach, 22
co-investigator, 27-9, 35, 96, 100, 103
collaborator, 15, 21, 27, 28, 38, 40, 110, 114
committee
    advisory, 23, 26, 27, 35
confidant, 22
confidentiality, 32, 53, 123, 128
conflict-of-interest, 122
consultant, 11, 21, 27, 28, 34, 35, 95, 96, 98, 100,
    102, 119, 121, 125, 129, 131
contract, 23, 32, 38, 95, 97, 100-2
cost escalation, 101
courses
    formal, 34
critics, 21, 54

D

Data and Safety Monitoring Board (DSMB), 11, 57,
    60, 62, 119, 121-3, 125, 130
data
    cleanup, 131
    coordinating center, 61, 119, 121, 125
    management core, 126, 127
    reporting guidelines, 131
    sharing, 125, 131
    storage, 104, 131
    verification, 60
database, 60, 81, 99, 103, 119, 123, 126-8
direct cost, 28, 95-7
distress, 63, 64, 77, 79, 112
DNA, 67, 68, 117
dog, 63-5, 69, 71, 74, 77
double-data entry, 124
Drug Enforcement Administration (DEA), 76

E

early termination, 60, 121, 125
editorial, 28
EEG, 65, 66, 68, 69, 76, 98, 104, 119
efficacy analyses, 128
EMG, 76
ENU, 66
environment, 15, 16, 19, 29, 37, 52, 63, 65, 70-2, 74, 75, 78, 80, 110, 112, 113
erudite, 24
ethics, 52, 54, 61, 62
euthanasia, 64, 73, 76, 79, 80, 82, 112
executive committee, 13, 120

F

faculty, 13, 15-7, 19, 22, 25, 26, 30, 42, 107, 108, 117
Fellow, 13, 16, 22, 23, 30, 33, 42, 96, 100
friend, 15, 21, 22, 38, 93
fruit fly, 66, 69
funding, 11, 15, 16-9, 21-4, 26-30, 37, 38, 42, 64, 74, 85, 91, 92, 95, 96, 101, 105, 107,108, 113, 117, 121

G

Gantt chart, 26
genetic
    engineering, 63, 69
    testing, 123
goals, 13, 16, 18, 26-8, 32, 35, 43, 60, 74, 75, 77, 110, 113, 121-3
grammar, 25
grant, 11, 13, 15-9, 21, 23, 25-30, 34, 37, 41, 42, 57, 58, 63, 64, 72-4, 80, 85, 86, 88, 89, 91, 92, 95, 96-9, 101, 105, 107-9, 112-8, 120-4
grant support, 16, 28
guide, 11, 13, 21, 23, 25, 30, 32, 57, 62, 63, 73, 74, 76, 80, 95, 101, 108, 117, 118

H

Health Insurance Portability and Accountability Act (HIPAA), 128
honors, 28, 35

human subjects, 17, 26, 52, 54-7, 61, 62, 110-2, 117
hypoxia, 70, 71, 79, 80, 82, 83, 87, 90, 91

I

ICSD-2, 63, 80
indirect cost, 95, 96, 98
industry, 13, 96, 121
informed consent, 50, 53, 56, 57, 123, 126
insomnia, 47, 57, 65, 70-2, 80, 82, 86
institution, 16-9, 23-5, 27, 28, 30, 37, 38, 74, 95-9, 101, 114, 121
Institutional Animal Care and Use Committee (IACUC), 63, 76, 77, 79, 80
Institute for Laboratory Animal Research (ILAR), 63, 73, 74, 76, 77, 82
Institutional Review Board (IRB), 52, 53, 122, 123, 129, 130
instrument addiction, 24
Integrated Review Group, 107
interim analyses, 125
internet, 17, 114, 125, 127, 128
investigator
    young, 11, 21-30

K

KO mice, 63, 66, 72

L

letter of support, 28, 104, 108

M

manual of operations, 120, 123, 126, 128, 129
megalomaniac, 24
mentee, 21-5, 27, 32
mentor, 11, 15-7, 21-7, 29, 30, 32, 37, 38, 42, 85, 114
mentor-mentee relationship, 22
mentorship contract, 32
mice, 63, 65-9, 71, 72, 78, 80, 81, 83
modular budget, 95, 98
monitoring, 11, 53, 56, 57, 60, 62, 64, 69, 75, 76, 78, 79, 103, 104, 111, 119, 121, 122, 124, 125, 127, 129

mRNA, 68
mutagenesis, 66, 69, 80

N

narcolepsy, 63, 65-7, 70, 71, 80, 81, 86
National Heart, Lung and Blood Institute (NHLBI), 11, 13, 16, 17, 30, 86, 119
National Institutes of Health (NIH), 11, 13, 16, 17, 23, 25, 27-30, 37, 42, 57, 63, 64, 73, 74, 80, 82, 85, 86, 92, 95-7, 99, 101, 104, 105, 107, 110-8, 120-2, 125, 131
NIH program officer, 120, 121, 125
no-cost extension, 101
NREM, 63, 65, 78, 83

O

Office of Animal Care and Use (OACU), 73
occupational health, 72, 73
Office of Laboratory Animal Welfare (OLAW), 73, 80, 112
operations core, 120, 125-7

P

pain, 64, 75-7, 79, 82, 112
participant education, 129
peer review, 15, 16, 26, 29, 35, 38, 107, 110, 113, 114, 116-8, 121
perseverance, 25
personnel training, 122, 126
pharmacology, 69
physician-observer, 119, 130
PLMS, 70, 71
position, 16, 21, 23, 28, 30, 33, 35, 41, 42, 55, 79, 121
primary outcomes, 39, 41, 121
primates, 64, 65, 68, 69, 74, 77, 82
principal investigator, 11, 17, 35, 45, 72, 96, 100, 102, 104, 107, 110, 119, 120, 122, 124, 125, 130
Program Officer, 18, 107, 108, 113, 119, 120-2, 125
project director, 120, 124
protocol, 41, 42, 45, 50, 53, 55-7, 59, 60, 72, 75, 77, 79, 102, 103, 114, 117, 116-26, 128-30
protocol violations, 122, 130

publication and presentation committee, 125, 127, 131
publications, 15, 24, 27, 28, 34, 35, 89, 103, 131
PubMed Central, 28

Q

quality assurance, 119, 121, 123, 124, 126, 127, 130
quality assurance supervisor, 124, 127, 130
quality control, 38, 60, 61, 103, 121, 124-7
quality control committee, 124, 127
Quantitative Trait Loci (QTL), 66, 67, 72, 81

R

randomization, 46, 47, 50, 51, 59, 61, 62, 122, 123, 126-8
rat, 65, 67, 70, 71, 78, 79, 81, 83
recruitment, 15, 56, 57, 101, 102, 104, 111, 120-4, 127, 130
REM, 65, 67, 69, 71, 78, 78, 81, 83
research, 11, 13, 15-9, 21-35, 37, 40-7, 52-7, 61-9, 72-7, 79, 80, 82, 85, 95-9, 101-5, 107-12, 117, 126
research design, 43, 46, 53, 111
research training, 16, 19, 29, 32, 34, 107
Resident, 23, 29
Restraint, 64, 76, 77, 82
Retention, 15, 57, 123, 124, 127, 130
RLS, 70-2
RNA, 66, 68, 81, 117
RNAi, 68
role model, 22, 23, 32

S

SAE, 129
Safety Officer, 130
Scientific Review Officer, 107, 109, 113
scientific writing, 25
screening, 34, 44, 66, 122, 123, 129
SD (sleep deprivation), 39, 44, 66, 72, 78, 79, 82
secondary outcomes, 128, 129
servers, 125
site
    coordinator, 120
    director, 11, 120
    visit, 60, 61, 122, 124

sleep, 11, 13, 17, 33, 34, 37, 39, 44, 46, 47, 53, 54, 59, 62-72, 75-83, 86, 87, 90, 92, 96, 98-104, 107, 108, 117, 119, 124, 126, 127, 129, 131

sleep apnea, 33, 39, 44, 47, 59, 62, 71, 71, 83, 86, 87, 90

sleep disorders, 13, 17, 33, 63, 34, 70-2, 80, 102, 108

Sleep Research Society (SRS), 11, 13

sponsor, 22, 34, 57, 99

statistical analysis, 43, 60, 70, 126, 128

statistics, 34, 40, 41, 61, 90, 128

steering committee, 61, 119-21, 123, 125, 129

study closeout, 120, 131

study design, 53, 70, 72, 126

study organization, 119, 120

study section, 38, 63, 85, 86, 88, 92, 93, 107-10, 112-5

support
   departmental, 29
   institutional, 29
   other, 29
   research, 15, 28, 35

surgery, 56, 64, 76, 77

SWS, 65

T

teacher, 21, 32

theorist, 25

time
   protected, 15, 16, 24-6, 29, 30
   management, 24

timeline, 27, 27, 72, 119, 121, 123, 129, 130, 131

trainee, 13, 25, 26, 28-30, 33, 37, 99

training
   grant, 23, 25-7, 29, 30
   matrix, 23, 33

traps, 21, 23

U

USDA, 76, 82

V

Vertebrae Animal Section (VAS), 63, 64, 80

vertebrate animals, 73, 82, 111, 112

veterinary care, 64, 74, 75, 77, 112

W

Web site, 17, 18, 25, 63, 73, 74, 85, 114, 118, 122, 124, 126, 128

Y

Young Investigators Forum, 13

Z

zebra fish, 63, 65, 66, 69